I0902079

Arado 232

The Luftwaffe's Combat Zone Transport Aircraft in World War II

David Myhra

Schiffer Military History
Atglen, PA

Acknowledgments

Dipl.-Ing. Karl Kössler - selected photographs from his published work, "Arado Ar 232 'Tatzelwurm' der erste Kampfzon-Transporter de Welt," *Jet & Prop Magazine*, January 1996, and "Schleppversuche mit Lastenglern," *Jet & Prop Magazine*, February 1996.
Mario Merino - computer generated digital images of the proposed Henschel Flugzeug transporter project.
Günter Sengfelder - photographs of his scratch-built, large, fine scale Arado Ar 232 model.

Book Design by: Joseph M. Riggio Jr.

Library of Congress Catalog Number: 2002108801

Printed in China.
ISBN: 0-7643-1665-6

We are interested in hearing from authors with book ideas on related topics.

Published by Schiffer Publishing Ltd.
4880 Lower Valley Road
Atglen, PA 19310
Phone: (610) 593-1777
FAX: (610) 593-2002
E-mail: Schifferbk@aol.com.
Visit our web site at: www.schifferbooks.com
Please write for a free catalog.
This book may be purchased from the publisher.
Please include $3.95 postage.
Try your bookstore first.

In Europe, Schiffer books are distributed by:
Bushwood Books
6 Marksbury Avenue
Kew Gardens
Surrey TW9 4JF
England
Phone: 44 (0) 20 8392-8585
FAX: 44 (0) 20 8392-9876
E-mail: Bushwd@aol.com.
Free postage in the UK. Europe: air mail at cost.
Try your bookstore first.

Arado Ar 232

Introduction

In 1933 the German airline *Lufthansa* introduced the exceptionally well built *Junkers Ju 52/3m* general purpose transport. Powered by three radial engines, the corrugated all-metal constructed transport reliably served the German airline, carrying passengers and goods throughout the world. As a passenger aircraft, it could carry up to fifteen passengers. Then, around autumn of 1939, with wartime conditions existing in *Nazi* Germany, the aging *Junkers Ju 52/3m* (*3m* meant 3 motored) was converted to carry troops, supplies, paratroopers, and was even used as a bomber. Something better was needed. However, there was no flying transport capable of entering and leaving a combat zone when the only airstrip available was a rough airfield or no airfield at all...fields of grass, or even a plowed farm field.

In autumn 1939, the *Technische Amt* of the *Reichsluftfahrtministerium* (*RLM*), or German Air Ministry, issued specifications for a general purpose transport to replace the *Junkers Ju 52/3m*. It must:

• Have the ability to operate in combat zones with rough ground and non-airfield conditions;
• Be able to carry supplies close to the front;
• Be powered by twin *BMW 801MA* 14-cylinder 1,600 horsepower air-cooled radial engines;
• Have retractable tricycle landing gear;
• Have a rear loading capability with a truck-height floor level for easy loading and unloading;
• Have a hydraulically lowered rear cargo door operable during flight...to off-load parachutists;
• Have a remote hydraulically operated nose cannon;
• Have a fuselage ceiling-mounted overhead sliding loading crane;
• Have cannon locations at the nose, rear, and upper fuselage;
• Have a rapid on and off cargo loading time;
• Have a short takeoff and landing capability;
• Have an attachment device to tow cargo gliders;
• Have an attachment for rocket-assisted takeoff devices;
• Be capable of operations in varying climates, such as North Africa and the Arctic.

The *RLM's Technische Amt* sent the design specifications to only two German aircraft manufacturers: *Arado Flugzeugwerke GmbH* and *Henschel Flugzeugwerke GmbH*. Both companies responded with a rectangular box-like, all-metal, semi monocoque cargo-carrying container hung beneath a shoulder high wing. As a result, the proposed designs did not look anything like the rugged passenger-like *Junker Ju 52/3m*, which they were attempting to replace. The *Junkers Ju 52/3m* had a box-like square door in the fuselage side, plus a rectangular door in the roof of the fuselage. Finally, both aircraft companies proposed carrying the tail assembly...twin booms from *Henschel Flugzeug* and a single tail boom from *Arado Flugzeug*. Furthermore, *Arado Flugzeug* proposed a truly innovative landing gear which would allow their plane to be a real combat zone tactical transport, with the ability to safely cross over ditches as wide as five feet. *Arado Flugzeug* suggested the use of a transitional tricycle landing gear, along with a multi-wheel static undercarriage involving 11 rows of 22 small idler wheels statically mounted beneath the fuselage on its centerline.

Arado Flugzeugwerke's proposed *Arado Ar 232*'s main undercarriage consisted of a tricycle semi-retractable levered-suspension nosewheel and an inward-retracting single-wheel main landing gear. Another innovation on the *Arado Ar 232* was that its tricycle landing gear could be compressed during loading and unloading, and then raised up so that the idler wheels cleared the runway for takeoff. Chief architect for the *Arado Ar 232* project was *Wilhelm van Nes*, and design supervisor was *Hans Rebeski*.

Luftwaffe fighter ace *Walter Blume* during WWI and shown wearing his *Pour le Mérite.*

Walter Blume during WWII and shown wearing his dress National Socialism uniform, along with his *Pour le Mérite.* He assumed technical directorship of *Arado Flugzeugwerke* in 1932 after the aircraft company was taken over by Nazi Germany and turned it into a state owned aircraft factory.

Walter Blume seen in the 1950s. He was born in 1896.

Walter Blume in the early 1960s. He died in Germany on March 7, 1964, age 68 years.

The legendary *Junkers Ju 52/3m* transport. It would be *Walter Blume's* goal to replace this flying machine with his state-of-the-art *Arado Ar 232A* combat zone transport.

The tri-motor *Junkers Ju 52/3m* was Germany's very reliable commercial/military transport, and it remained in service in many countries long after WWII.

The aging *Junkers Ju 52/3m* transport needed an easier way to load and offload cargo, such as this mini auto, through a removal/hinged hatch on its roof. A very delicate job at best. *Walter Blume* would design his twin engine *Arado Ar 232A* with a rear cargo ramp for easy loading and offloading, allowing a *Volkswagen* auto, for example, to be driven in and backed out of the *Arado Ar 232.* Think of the time it would save by just eliminating the lifting crane and its crew...to load and later to unload.

A port side view of the corrugated metal fuselage of a *Junkers Ju 52/3m*. Its top-loading roof hatch/door can be seen in the open position. Very small and very awkward.

Soldiers boarding and waiting to board a *Junkers Ju 52/3m*. *Walter Blume* instructed his designer team that he wanted to double the number of soldiers carried by the old *Ju 52/3m* transport in his new *Arado Ar 232* transport.

Willy Messerschmitt **offered the** ***Luftwaffe*** **his six piston engined heavy transport. That was the problem. It got to be so heavy that the** ***Me 323 "Gigant,"*** **or Giant, came to be the largest flying machine to be placed into service with the** ***Luftwaffe*****. It was so large that it required tow aircraft to help it lift off the runway.** ***Walter Blume*** **believed that his** ***Arado Ar 232*** **was the logical way to a better transport.**

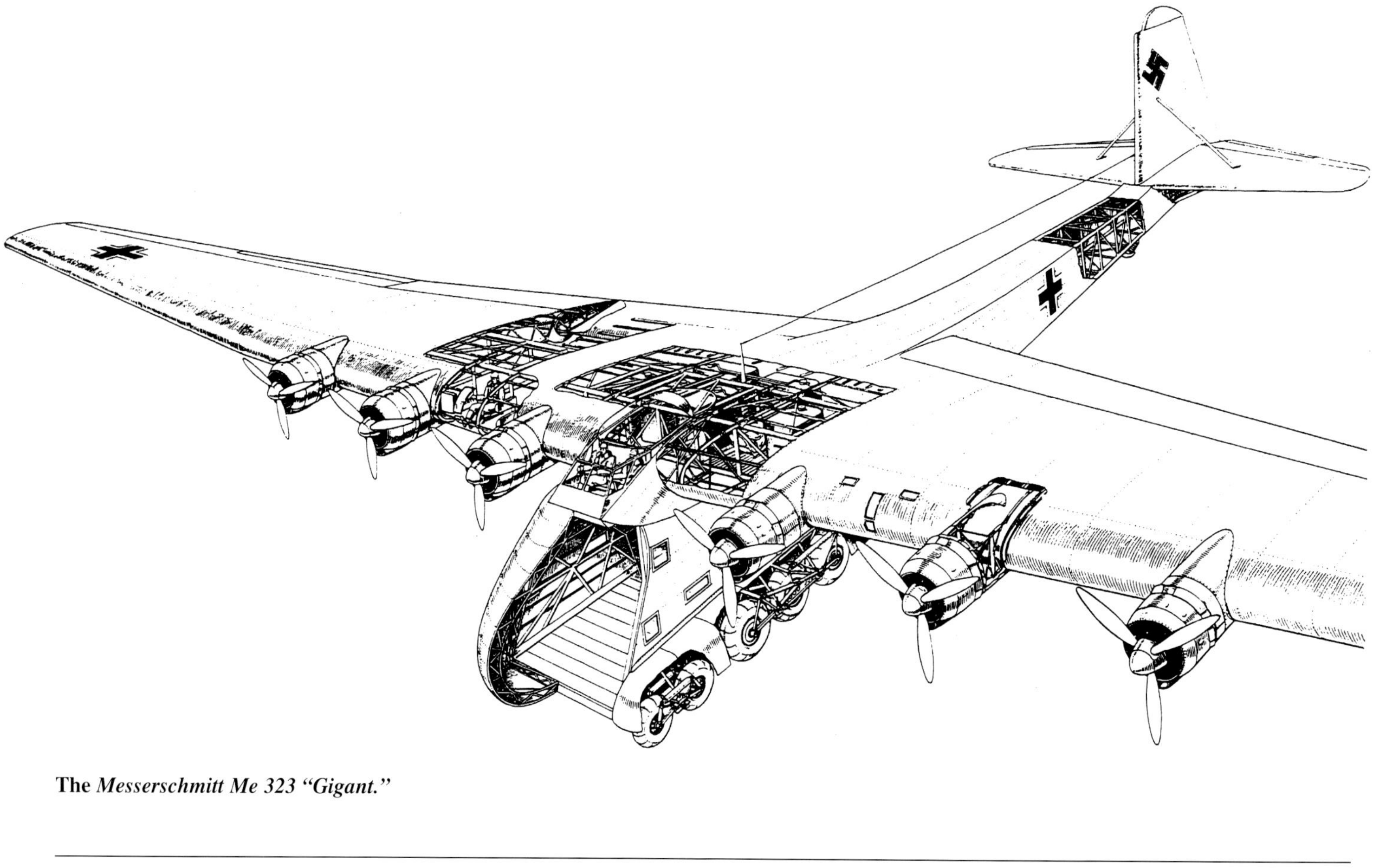

The ***Messerschmitt Me 323 "Gigant."***

A *Messerschmitt Me 323* **loading a wheeled heavy artillery piece through its open nose cargo doors via a tracked prime mover. All this the** *Me 323* **could accommodate, but the flying machine was too slow, too heavy, and it could not land well on unimproved fields with its typical landing gear.** *Walter Blume* **would see to it that his** *Arado Ar 232* **transport could land on most surfaces...even landing fields with trenches up to 5 feet wide.**

Arado Ar 232A Design Specifications

• **Wingspan** - 105 feet [32.0 meters];
• **Wing surface area** - [135.0 meters];
• **Length** - 77 feet [23.5 meters];
• **Height, overall** - 21 feet 7 inches [6.6 meters];
• **Engines**: 2x*BMW 801MA* 14-cylinder air-cooled radial engines rated at 1,600 horsepower each;
• **Speed, maximum** - 210 miles/hour at 18,045 feet altitude [338 kilometers/hour at 5.5 kilometers];
• **Speed, maximum cruising speed** - not available;
• **Range, normal** - not available;
• **Climb to 6,560 feet** - not available;
• **Climb to 13,120 feet** - not available;
• **Climb to 19,685 feet** - not available;
• **Service ceiling** - not available;
• **Weight, empty equipped** - 36,597 pounds;
• **Weight, normal loaded** - 46,584 pounds;

Prototypes and Pre-Series Machines Constructed

• ***Arado Ar 232 A-0 (V1)*** **-** radio call code *GH+GN* was flown for the first time in early summer 1941. Powered by two *BMW 801MA* 14-cylinder air-cooled radial piston engines. No defensive armament had been installed. This flying machine, undergoing flight testing, was pressed into service to airlift battle wounded troops from the combat zone of the 6th Army at Stalingrad. The pilot became disoriented enroute in a snow storm over Poland and crashed, killing all crewmembers.

• ***Arado Ar 232 A-1 (V2)*** **-** radio call code *VD+YA*—the first *"A"* prototype to be flown with its full compliment of defensive armament, which included:

• one 13 mm *MG 131* cannon with 500 rounds positioned to fire through the cockpit nose;

• one 20 mm *MG 151* cannon in a hydraulically-operated turret over the forward fuselage;

Willy Messerschmitt wanted his _Me 323 "Gigant"_ transport to replace the aging _Junkers Ju 52/3m_. _Walter Blume_ believed that his _Arado Ar 232_ transport would be the _Luftwaffe's_ transport of choice. The caption in this _Messerschmitt AG_ magazine ad reads..."Already today the German aircraft industry is performing through the building of the large room vehicle _Messerschmitt Me 323 'Gigant,'_ a contribution for the international goods traffic on the air streets of the future."

Walter Blume's Arado Ar 232A **transport...everything the** ***Luftwaffe*** **needed for a combat zone transport and nothing that it didn't. This flying machine would be the first combat zone transport in the world. Scale model and photographed by** ***Günter Sengfelder.***

• one *MG 131* cannon positioned above the loading ramp door;
• up to eight *MG 53* infantry *Mauser* rifle machine guns mounted to fire out through openings in the cargo bay windows.

This flying machine, also undergoing flight testing yet equipped with a ski instead of its idler wheels, was flown to Zhitomir, USSR, in January 1943, where it landed in nearly two feet of snow. It was later used in the evacuation of Sevastopol, USSR, and is thought to be the last *Luftwaffe* flying machine to leave Stalingrad alone or without heavy fighter escort.

• ***Arado Ar 232 A-2 (V3)*** **-** radio call code *VD+YC*—The first four engine version of the *Arado Ar 232*; flight testing began in May 1942.

• ***Arado Ar 232 A-3 (V4)*** - no known radio call code, but considered to be the first of the eight pre-series four engine *Arado Ar 232B-O* transports constructed. The *Arado Ar 232 V4* was modified to carry four engines (*BMW-Bramo 323R-2* "*Fafnir,*" 9-cylinder radial engines). To accommodate the four engines with their individual 1,200 takeoff horsepower, the *Arado Ar 232B-1*'s wing center section was lengthened by 5 feet 7 inches.

• ***Arado Ar 232 A-4 (V5)*** **-** no reliable data available.
• ***Arado Ar 232 A-5 (V6)*** **-** no reliable data available.
• ***Arado Ar 232 A-6 (V7)*** **-** no reliable data available.

• ***Arado Ar 232 A-7 (V8)*** - (also known as *Arado Ar 232 B-5*) - Made its maiden flight in May 1943. It is believed to have been experimentally fitted out with four French *Gnôme-Rhône 14M* 14-cylinder air cooled radial engines rated at 700 takeoff horsepower. Internal fuel tankage was increased to 1,100 gallons from 595 gallons. It is known that this experimental transport was used for meteorological duties operating out of Banak, Norway.

• ***Arado Ar 232 A-8 (V9)*** **-** no reliable data available.
• ***Arado Ar 232 A-9 (V10)*** **-** no reliable data available.

• ***Arado Ar 232 A-10 (V11)*** **-** radio call code *TC+EG.* Flown extensively out of Banak, Norway. It is reported that its tricycle landing gear had been fixed in an open position and its idler wheels had been replaced by a single ski 26 feet 3 inches in length by 7 feet 11 inches wide. Lost on August 26, 1943, shortly after takeoff en route to Brandenburg from Norway after its starboard engine failed. As many as twenty individuals being transported to Brandenburg may have lost their lives.

Arado Ar 232 B Series Flying Machines

Oberst Siegfried Knemeyer of the German Air Ministry, believing that the *Luftwaffe* now had a successful combat zone transport with its twin engine *Arado Ar 232A*, made plans to put them into series production. However, the *BMW 801MA* 1,600 horsepower 14-cylinder radial was required by the *Focke-Wulf Fw 190* fighter, and none could be diverted to the *Ar 232A*. Thus, series production of the *Arado Ar 232* transport could not begin until a suitable radial engine was available. The engine that became available was the new *BMW-Bramo 323R-2* engine. However, this 9-cylinder radial

Walter Blume's Arado Ar 232A* combat zone transport could carry twice the amount of supplies of the *Junkers Ju 52/3m* and had a forward speed about 45 mph faster. Scale model and photographed by *Günter Sengfelder.

produced only 1,200 horsepower, making a twin engine *Arado Ar 232* powered by the *BMW-Bramo* unsuitable for its intended role as a combat zone transport. *Oberst Knemeyer's* solution was to equip the *Arado Ar 232* with four of the 1,200 horsepower *BMW-Bramo* engines and continue on with plans for its series production. This action on the part of *Knemeyer* came sort of as a blessing in disguise. The twin *BMW 801A* engined *Arado Ar 232A* was pretty much unable to stay aloft with only one engine operating. But with four *BMW-Bramo 323R-2*'s radial piston engines the *Arado Ar 232* obtained greater safety. In addition, the four *Bramos* shortened the transporter's takeoff run, gave it a little higher top speed, and reduced the time to gain flight altitude. *Oberst Knemeyer* re-designated the four-engine *Arado* transport as the *Arado Ar 232B*.

The *Arado Ar 232A* transport, seen here, had a cantilever mid-wing and a smooth skinned monocoque surface...unlike the corrugated skinned *Junkers Ju 52/3m*. Scale model and photographed by *Günter Sengfelder.*

This *Arado Ar 232A*, seen as it passes over the camera, was the only combat zone transporter with the ability to operate from rough airfields and carry goods and men right to the front lines, thanks to what *Arado Flugzeugwerke* called the "*Grendel*," or millipede...its secondary static landing gear consisting of 11 rows of 22 pneumatic tires. Scale model and photographed by *Günter Sengfelder.*

The amount of cargo the *Arado Ar 232A* could accommodate in its cargo bay (21.6 feet [6.6 meters] long, 7.6 feet [2.3 meters] wide, and 6.6 feet[2.0 meters] high) was considerable (about 10,000 pounds), as can be seen in this photograph. Two small autos, a *Junkers Jumo 004* turbojet engine, tires, and other miscellaneous items are seen in this picture. A fixed overhead loading crane was located in the cargo bay to reduce the need for an army of men to manhandle the heavier items. Scale model and photographed by *Günter Sengfelder.*

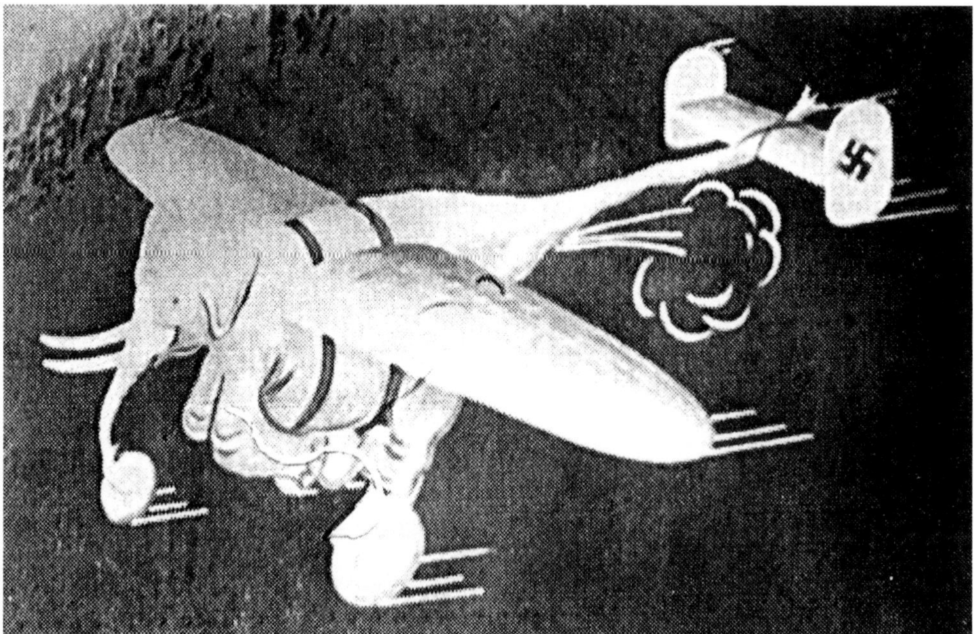

This "*elephant*" emblem was painted on the nose of *Arado Ar 232As*, and represented the flying combat zone transporter as a heavy hauler.

Feldwebel (Technical Sergeant) *Ernst Funk* shown in the pilot's seat of an *Arado Ar 232A*. Post war *Funk* instructed the RAF on piloting the four-engined *Arado Ar 232Bs.* Courtesy: *Dipl.-Ing. Karl Kössler,* "Arado Ar 232 'Tatzelwurm,' der erste Kampfzonen-Transporter de Welt," Jet & Prop, 1/96, page 58.

Oberfeldwebel (Master Sergeant) *Max Limbrecht*, one of the most experienced pilots of the *Arado Ar 232* combat zone transport. Courtesy: *Dipl.-Ing. Karl Kössler, "Schleppversuche mit Lastenseglern," Jet & Prop,* 2/96, page 41.

The *Arado Ar 232A* as seen from its port rear side. Its hydraulically operated loading ramp is down and equipment and supplies are being loaded. In order to achieve an acceptable landing speed the *Ar 232A's* wings were fitted with electrically activated "*Arado* traveling flaps," or "*Arado* area-increasing flaps" along their entire span. Scale model and photographed by *Günter Sengfelder.*

Arado Ar 232A radio call code *TC+EF* as seen from its starboard side nose. Its tricycle landing gear oleo struts are in the full lowered position so that each of its 22 "*Grendel*" pneumatic tires are on the tarmac, too, helping to reduce the weight on its tricycle landing gear, especially during landing on rough fields.

A full port side view of an *Arado Ar 232A* radio call code *TC+EF*. This combat zone transport carried a crew of four men: pilot, co-pilot, and two machine gun operators. Notice that its 22 pneumatic tires are well off the tarmac, meaning that its tricycle landing gear is in the full up position. Scale model and photographed by *Günter Sengfelder.*

A ground level photo of an *Arado Ar 232A* combat zone transport as seen from its starboard side. It was known by several nicknames, including "*Tausendfüsser*," meaning millipede, and "*Tatzelwurm*"...a mythical alpine dragon, because of its 22 pneumatic tires statically fixed beneath the fuselage to keep ground pressure low on its tricycle landing gear.

The *Arado Ar 232A V1*...the first of the "*A*" series prototype seen as it begins its takeoff roll during one of its initial flight tests in early summer 1941. Notice that the oleo struts of its tricycle landing gear are fully extended, and when fully extended raise the 11 rows of 22 pneumatic wheels high off the surface, whether it be a plowed field, grass, or tarmac.

A rare photo of an *Arado Ar 232A* seen in flight passing over the railroad tracks near the cities of Malge and Brandenburg. Notice the *Ar 232A's* slender tail boom, which carried dual vertical fins with attached hinged rudders. The height of the boom was designed so that it would not interfere with the loading and off-loading of cargo from its rear fold down door.

The *Arado Ar 232A-010* from *Westa 5* seen on the ground in Banak, Norway, in July 1943, as seen from its nose port side. On its side nose can be seen an emblem...not the usual "elephant" emblem, but a shield containing its *Staffel* emblem. Courtesy: *"Arado: History of an Aircraft Company," Jörg Armin Kranzhoff*, Schiffer Publishing, Atglen, PA, 1997.

A similar view of the *Arado Ar 232A-010* as seen above. This combat zone transport was flown by *Oberleutnant Schütze* of *Westa 5,* Banak, Norway. Notice that this flying machine carries *Westa 5's* shield/emblem. Its propellers were *VDM* variable pitch with 14 foot [4.3 meter] diameters!

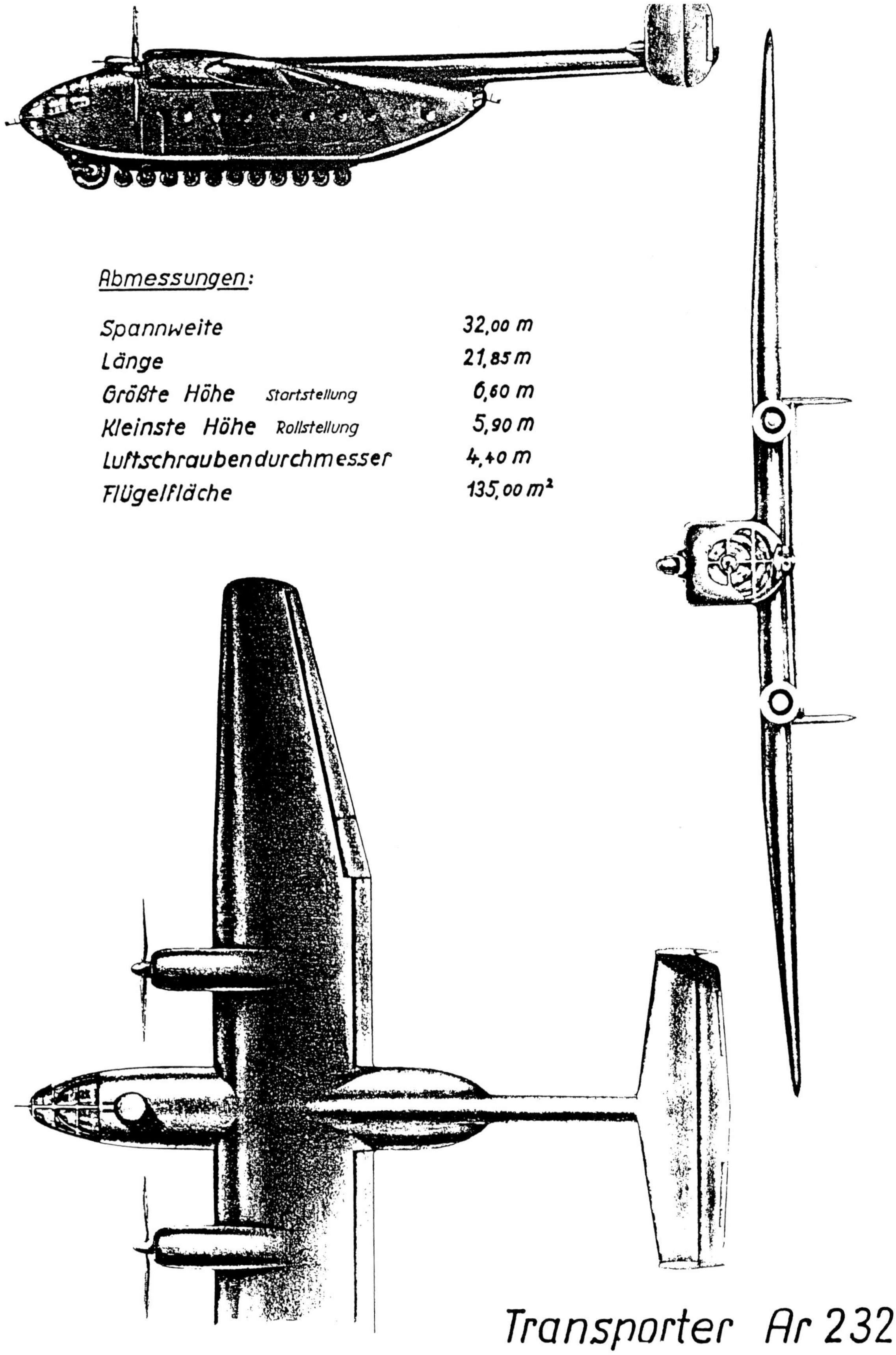

A three-view illustration of the *Arado Ar 232A* from Arado flugzeugwerke.

The *Arado Ar 232A-006* radio call code *LS+BR*. It is shown at Eger, May 1944, perhaps back from delivery duties on the Eastern Front. The "*elephant*" emblem on its nose can be clearly seen.

A very nice port side photo of *Arado Ar 232A-003* radio call code *VD+YC*. Pilot *Oberleutnant Meltzer* lost his life when this flying machine crashed at Schönwalde. Beneath the port wing's trailing edge by the port main gear can be seen three individuals. Their small size provides perspective to the size of this *Arado* combat zone transporter.

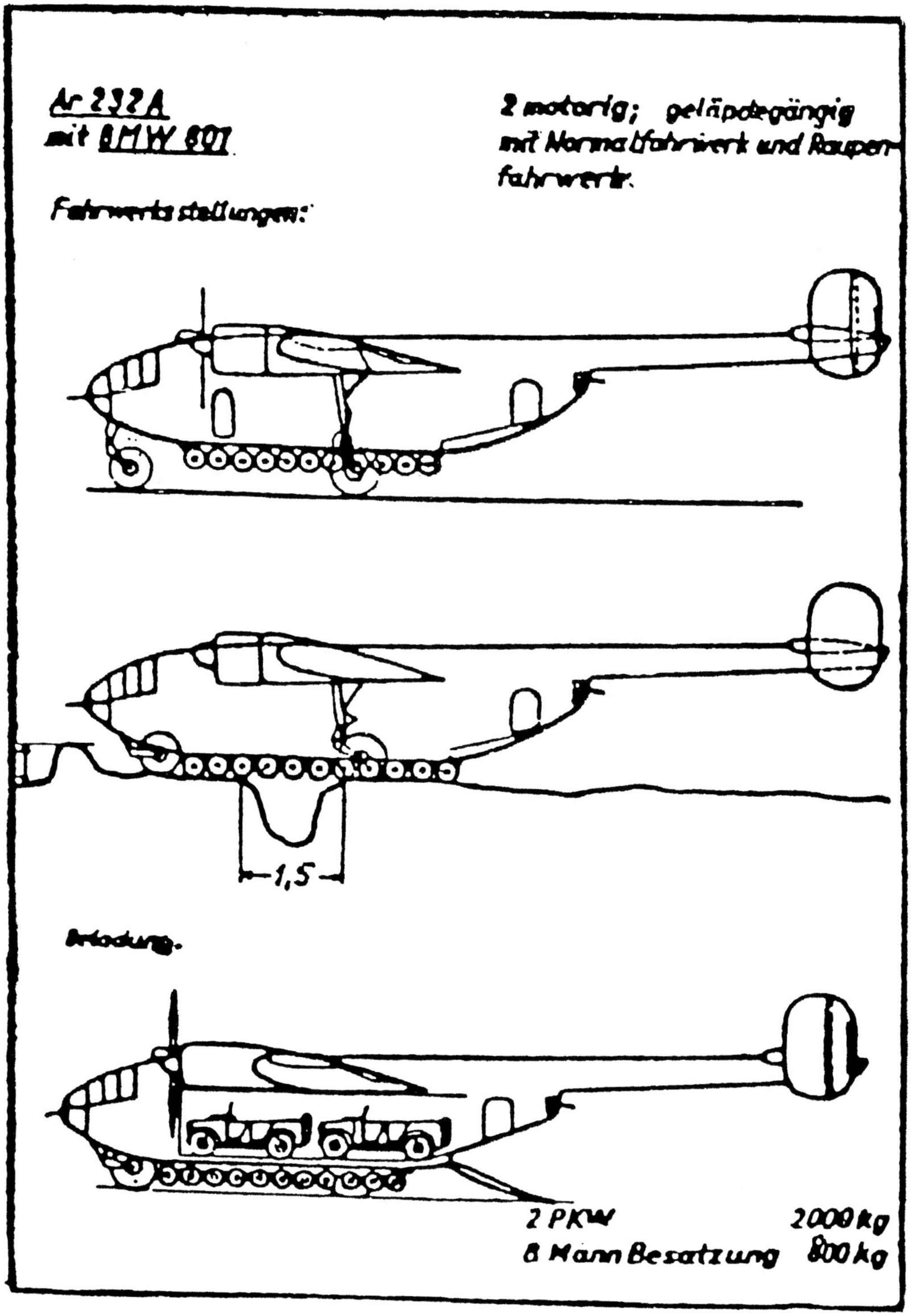

An illustration by *Arado Flugzeugwerke* graphically showing how their *Arado Ar 232A* with its 11 rows of dual pneumatic wheels beneath the fuselage is able to cross over trenches up to five feet [1.52 meters] wide.

Arado Ar 232A V1, radio call code *GH+GN* and seen prior to painting and national insignia in early 1941 as it was undergoing flight testing as a prototype for the *Ar 232A* series. It was powered by twin *BMW 801MA* radial piston engines. Only two prototypes were constructed: *GH+GN* and *YD+YA*, and *Ar 232A V2* radio call code *YD+YA*.

The *Arado Ar 232A V1* radio call code *GH+GN* now shown with a dark camouflaged paint job, including an oversized swastika on its starboard side vertical stabilizer with hinged rudder.

The results when *Arado Ar 232A-08* was destroyed in a landing accident on December 14, 1944, when it collided with a *Junkers Ju 88* at Jesau. For some unknown reason its *Staffel* emblem on the forward fuselage was painted over before this photo was taken—perhaps to eliminate embarrassment to *Staffel* members.

***Arado Ar 232A V1* radio call code *GH+GN* as viewed on the ground featuring its port side and a good view of its port *BMW 801MA* radial piston engine. Seen prior to painting and national insignia. This prototype for the *Ar 232A* series was being flight tested in early 1941.**

Arado Ar 232A V1 radio call code *GH+GN*. Prototype for the A series. This photo is from the time it had started its flight trials. No paint and no national insignia. Initially plans called for the *Arado Ar 232A* to be used in operations in North Africa and the Arctic.

A profile of an *Arado Ar 232A* (radio call code unknown) in flight as seen from its starboard side. Although a poor quality photo, this *Ar 232A's* 11 rows of dual pneumatic tires statically fixed in caterpillar fashion seen beneath its fuselage are nicely presented.

The *Arado Ar 232A-010* seen after a landing mishap at South Cap of Spitzbergen. It appears that the *Ar 232A's* starboard main wheel collapsed, and the transport fell over on its starboard wing. Notice the individual who has crawled out on the *Ar 232A's* port wing tip and how small he appears.

***Arado Ar 232B* Design Specifications**

- **Wingspan -** 110 feet [33.5 meters];
- **Wing Surface Area** - 1,534 feet squared [142.5 meters squared];
- **Length -** 77 feet [23.5 meters];
- **Height, overall -** 21 feet 7 inches [6.6 meters];
- **Engines -** 4x*BMW-Bramo 323R-2* "*Fafnir,*" 9-cylinder air-cooled radial engines rated at 1,200 horsepower each;
- **Speed, maximum -** 191 miles/hour at 13,120 feet altitude [308 kilometers/hour at 4 kilometers altitude];
- **Speed, maximum cruising speed -** 179 miles/hour at 6,560 feet altitude [288 kilometers/hour at 2 kilometers altitude];
- **Range, normal -** 830 miles at 158 miles/hour [1,335 kilometers];
- **Climb to 6,560 feet -** 7 minutes;
- **Climb to 13,120 feet -** 15.8 minutes;
- **Climb to 19,685 feet -** 27 1/2 minutes;
- **Service ceiling -** 22,640 feet [6,900 meters];
- **Weight, empty equipped -** 28,175 pounds [12,780 kilograms];
- **Weight, normal loaded -** 44,090 pounds [20,000 kilograms];

Eight *Arado Ar 232B* pre-production four engine transports are known to have been constructed, designated as *Ar 232B-O*, although ten are thought to have been ordered by *Siegfried Knemeyer*. The eight *Arado Ar 232B-Os...V4* through *V11*, include:

• ***Arado Ar 232 B-O* (*V4*)** - Formerly known as the twin engine *Ar 232A*. It was retained by *Arado Flugzeugwerke* for ongoing airframe testing, including replacement of the existing control surfaces with one made out of wood. This four-motored flying machine was also experimentally fitted with a boundary layer control (BLC) system, with air from the wing's leading edge being sucked into the interior by hydrogen peroxide driven pumps and then being blown out over the wing's trailing edge. Later, this prototype was utilized by *Arado Flugzeugwerke* to serve as a supply transport for its twin turbojet powered *Arado Ar 234B* reconnaissance/bomber and the four turbojet powered *Ar 234C* "Englander Bomber." At war's end the *Ar 232B-O V4* ended up at the RAF-Farnborough and is believed to have been scrapped in early 1947.

This *Arado Ar 232A-010* radio call code *TC+EG* from *Westa 5,* Banak, Norway, appears to have landed in soft or sandy ground, as evidenced by the tracks its landing gear have made behind as its gear sank down. It had landed on Bear Island, Norway, on August 7, 1943.

A direct ground level nose-on view into the cockpit of an *Arado Ar 232A*. Situated above and behind the cockpit is the turret for the single manned *MG 81Z* cannon. A second *MG 81Z* cannon, remotely controlled, was located in the nose. The flying machine carried 1,600 rounds for this cannon. It nose wheel was large, and it appears that its oleo strut is fully retracted so that its 11 pair of fuselage mounted tires also touch the tarmac. Scale model and photographed by *Günter Sengfelder.*

1 10 Rumpfwerk Ar 232 A-O Flugzeug-Handbuch

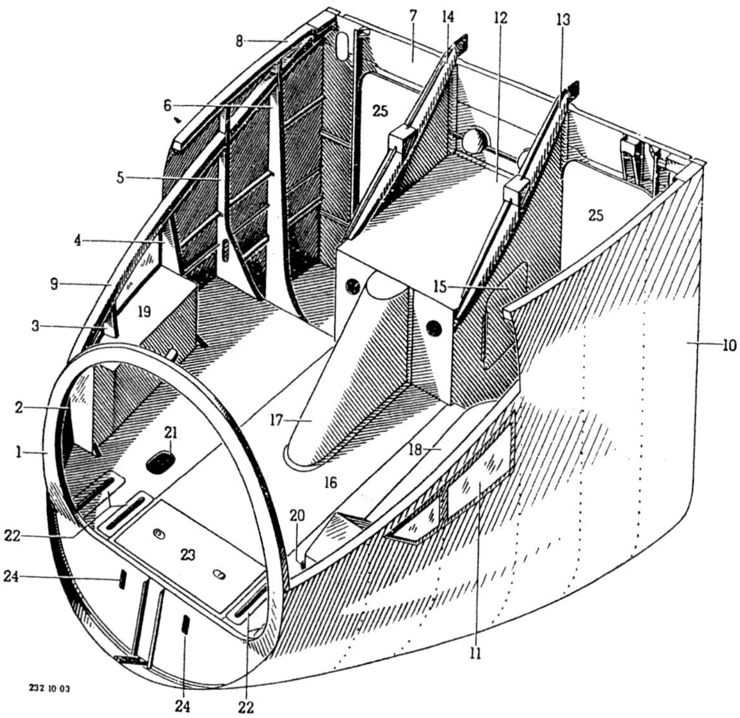

1–7 Spant 1 bis Spant 7
8 Vorderteil-Obergurt
9 Vorderteil-Untergurt
10 Beplankung zu den Halbschalen
11 Sichtfenster
12 Schützenstand
13 Linke Wange mit Auftritt
14 Rechte Wange mit Auftritt
15 Klappe im Schützenstand
16 Fußboden
17 Verkleidung für Bugradfederstrebe
18 Linke Bedienbank
19 Rechte Bedienbank
20 Durchgang für Führersteuersäule
21 Durchgang für Bordwartsteuersäule
22 Schlitze für Fußhebel
23 Gurtkastendeckel
24 Durchgänge für Gurtzuführung
25 Durchgang im Spant 7

Rumpfvorderteil (Führerraum)

An illustration from *Arado Flugzeugwerke* featuring form and layout of the nose section (*rumpfwerke*) from an *Arado Ar 232A-O*.

The spacious cockpit of an *Arado Ar 232A*. The round tube-like structure between the seats is for the nose wheel landing gear/strut. In its nose was mounted a single remotely controlled *MG 81Z* cannon with 1,000 rounds. Scale model and photographed by *Günter Sengfelder.*

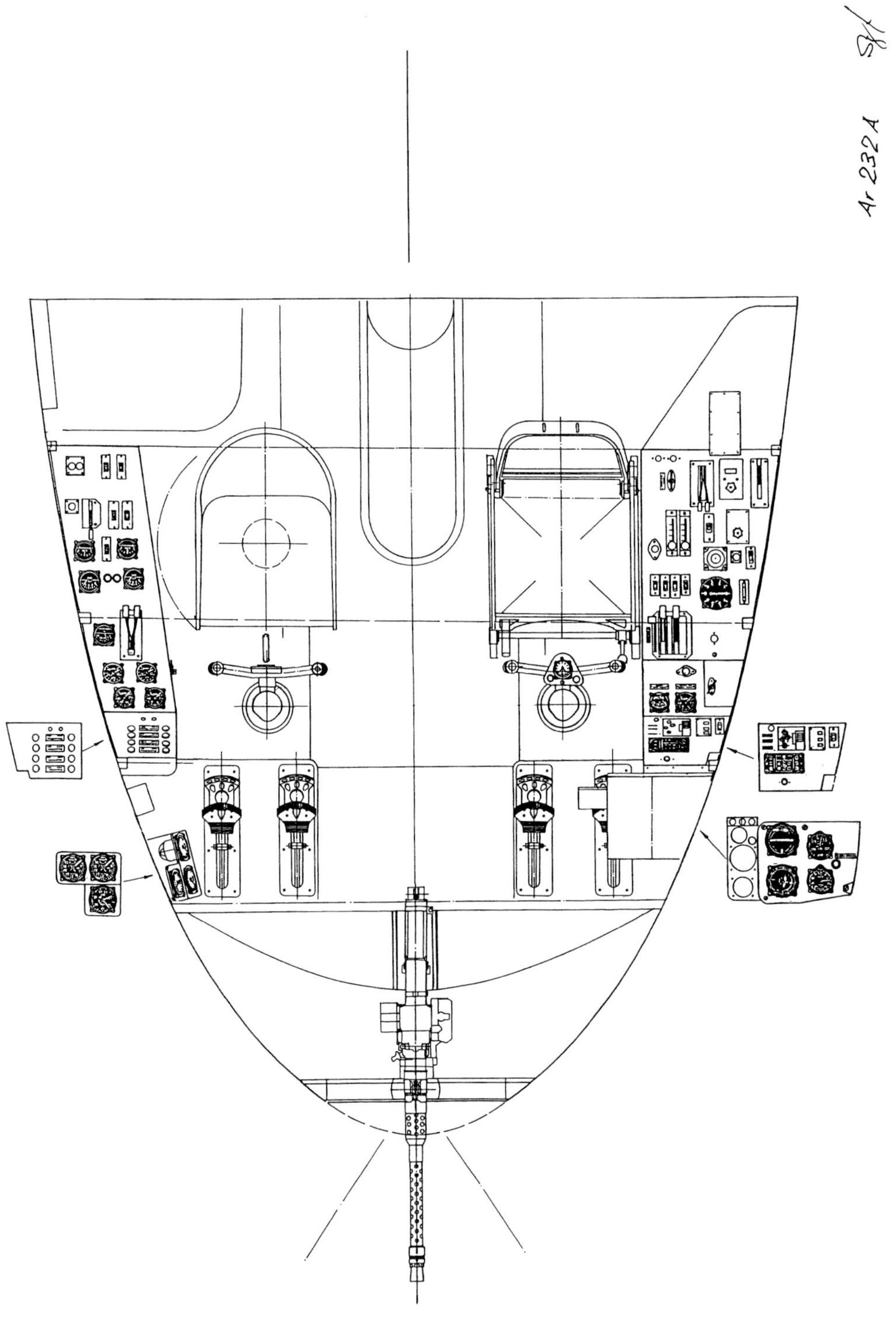

An illustration from *Arado Flugzeugwerke,* redrawn, features the cockpit layout and side instrument panels of an *Arado Ar 232A*.

Nose-on view of the *Arado Ar 232 V1* prototype. Notice that no cannons are featured either in the nose, or in a turret above and behind the cockpit. Notice, too, that the two gentlemen at the controls are wearing suits, white shirts, and neckties! The nose wheel oleo strut appears fully extended, and its welded steel tube structure is well presented.

A ground level view looking up at the *Arado* Ar *232A V1* prototype, its nose wheel, nose wheel gear, and window panels.

The nose wheel landing gear and oleo strut as seen from behind.

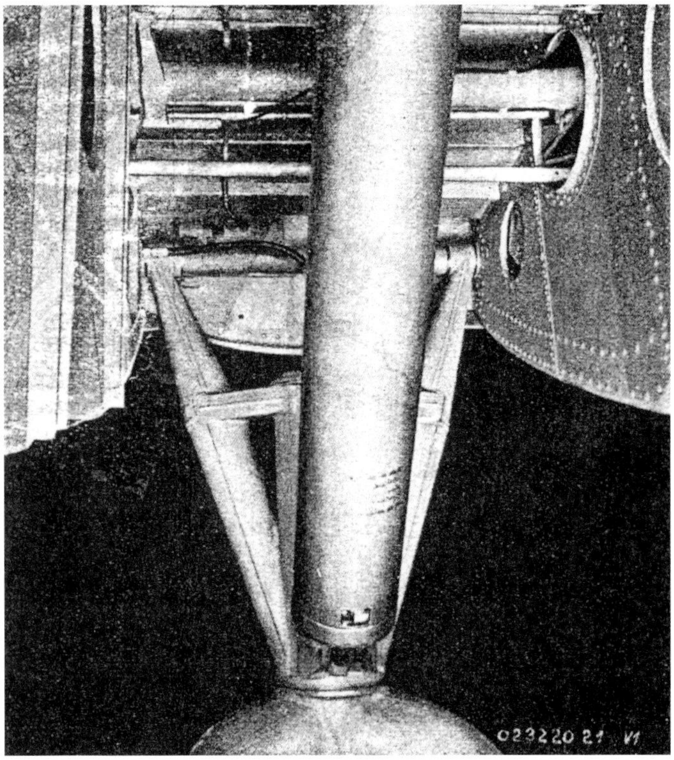

• ***Arado Ar 232 B-O*** **(*V5*)** - no reliable data available;
• ***Arado Ar 232 B-O*** **(*V6*)** - no reliable data available;
• ***Arado Ar 232 B-O*** **(*V7*)** - no reliable data available;

• ***Arado Ar 232 B-O*** **(*V8*)** - Fitted out with four French *Gnôme-Rhône 14M* 14-cylinder radial engines each rated at 700 horsepower for takeoff, first flight was in May 1943. Later put into service with *Westa 5* out of Banak, Norway, carrying out meteorological duties.

• ***Arado Ar 232 B-O*** **(*V9*)** - no reliable data available;
• ***Arado Ar 232 B-O*** **(*V10*)** - no reliable data available;

• ***Arado Ar 232 B-O*** **(*V11*)** - Served also with *Westa 5* out of Banak, Norway. Reportedly it underwent major landing gear modifications while with *Westa 5*. The main wheels were fixed in the extended position, while its 11 rows of tires were replaced by a single wooden ski measuring 26 feet 2 inches long and 7 feet 10 inches wide.

A new-looking *Arado Ar 232A* seen from its starboard side nose. Attempts have been made to camouflage this combat zone transporter. Featured, too, is the nose wheel, and immediately aft is the first of the 11 dual caterpillar-like landing wheels.

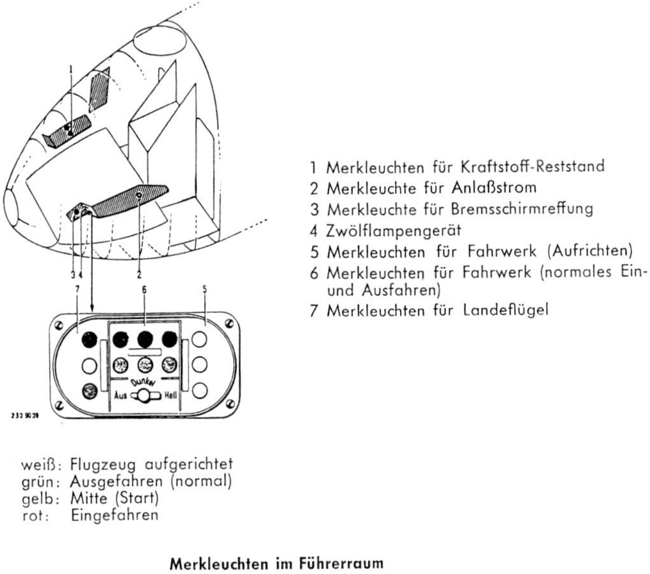

An illustration from *Arado Flugzeugbau*. The indicator lights located on the starboard side panel in the cockpit of an *Arado Ar 232A* feature fuel remaining and landing gear position.

A view of the cockpit of an *Arado Ar 232A* featuring the starboard side instrument panel.

In addition to the eight *Arado Ar 232B-O* pre-production examples produced, it is believed that between twenty and twenty-two additional series machines may have been constructed. If so, they were put to immediate use. However, very little reliable data survives. For example, *Arado Ar 232Bs* were used for transporting high-priority aircraft parts and assemblies. As many as six new *Arado Ar 232Bs* were handed over to the *Ergänzugs-Transport-Gruppe* of *14 Staffel* of *Transportgeschwader 4*. Another five new flying machines are believed to have been delivered to the secretive *Kampfgescher (Battle Wing) 200*, or *KG 200*. Post war one of *KG 200's Arado Ar 232Bs* with radio call code *A3+RB (IIKG 200)* was found at Eggebeck on July 14, 1945; it was ferried to RAF-Farnborough and was assigned Air Ministry number *AM 17*. *A3+RB* was placed on static display during Farnborough's German Aircraft Exhibition, and it is known to have been on the registry at Farnborough in April 1946. It was selected for museum storage by the RAF's Air Ministry Air Historical Branch, and was dismantled and transported to Sealand on September 19th of that year. By April 3, 1947, this *Arado Ar 232B* had been packaged (ten crates) for museum storage. This disassembled combat zone transport was not meant to be saved, however, because the flying machine disappeared, and the last known mention in official records is in November 1947. It is assumed that this *Arado Ar 232B* was disposed of in late 1947 or early 1948 due to a lack of storage space at Sealand.

Arado Ar 232Bs are known to have been involved in at least two *Kampfgeschwader 200* (*KG 200*) secret missions near war's end. Since *KG 200* are known to have taken part in many covert missions against the Allies they are the subject of much postwar speculation.

The starboard side all metal pilot's seat in the *Arado Ar 232A*, which has been rotated 180 degrees around to the navigation table.

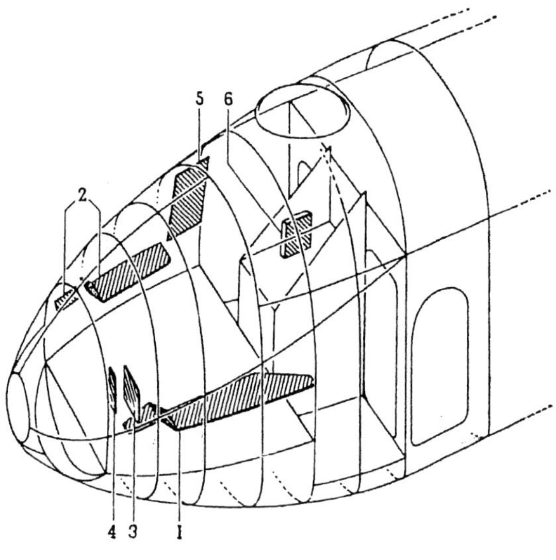

An illustration from *Arado Flugzeugbau* featuring the positions of several instrument panels in the cockpit of an *Arado Ar 232A*.

Anlage 13

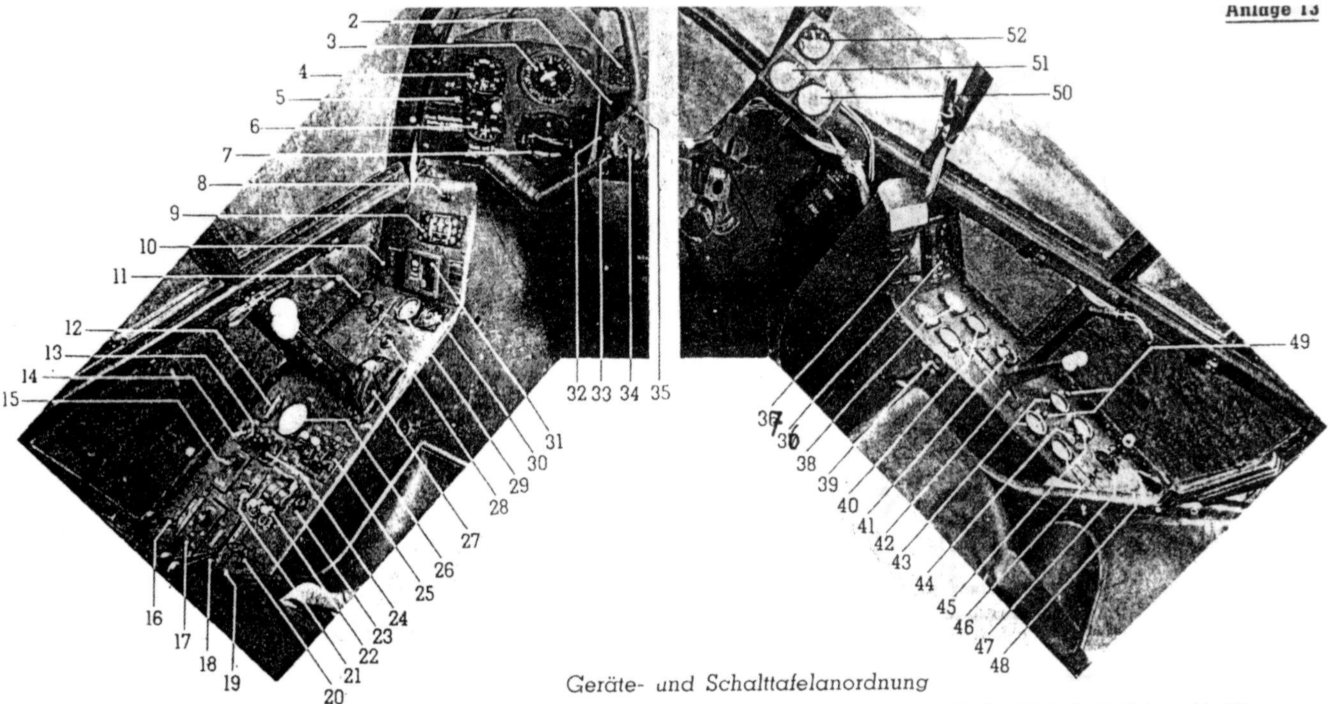

Geräte- und Schalttafelanordnung

1 Zielfluggerät
2 Variometer
3 Führerlochlerkompaß
4 Höhenmesser
5 Schauzeichen für Staurohrheizung
6 Fahrtmesser
7 Wendehorizont
8 Merkleuchte für Bremsschirmreffung
9 Zwölflampengerät
10 Schalter für Kurssteuerung
11 Bremsschirm-Notzug
12 Schieber für Deviationstabellen
13 Schalter für Deckenbeleuchtung
14 Verdunkler
15 FT-Fernbedienung
16 Behälterschalthebel
17 FT-Anschlußdose
18 Brandhahnhebel
19 Anlaßschalter (Starter)
20 Bremsschirmauslösung
21 Elt-Schalter für Scheinwerfer
22 Zündschalter
23 Netzausschalter
24 Dreiachsen-Trimmschalter
25 Handschalter für Luftschraubenverstellung
26 Dreiachsen-Trimmanzeiger
27 Gashebel nebst Feststellhebel
28 Druckknopf für Druckspeicherregelung
29 Druckmesser für Bremsanlage
30 Doppel-Steigungsanzeiger u. Landeflügel
31 Druckknöpfe für Fahrwerk~~betätigung~~
32 Anklemmvorrichtung für Notwendezeiger
33 Sprechknopf für Fu G 16
34 Borduhr
35 Elt-Schalter für Borduhrbeleuchtung
36 Druckknöpfe für ~~Landeflügelbetätigung (Fowler)~~ Absenken u. Aufrichten
37 Druckknöpfe für Fahrwerkbetätigung
38 Druckmesser für Kraftstoff u. Schmierstoff
39 Handgriff für Pedaleinstellung
40 Schmierstoff-Temperaturmesser
41 Außentemperaturmesser
42 Gashebel
43 Kraftstoff-Vorratsmesser
44 Elt-Schalter für Luftschrauben-Enteisung
45 Schmierstoffvorratsmesser
46 Elt-Schalter für Schmierstoffkühlung (Haubennasenring)
47 Hebel für Führerraumbeheizung
48 Elt-Schalter für Zylinderkühlung (Spreizklappe, Drosselring)
49 Merkleuchten für Kraftstoff-Reststand
50 Elt-Ferndrehzahlmesser
51 Elt-Ferndrehzahlmesser
52 Doppel-Ladedruckmesser

A poor quality panorama photo featuring the flight controls and flight instruments in the cockpit of an *Arado Ar 232A*.

The port side instrument panel in the *Arado Ar 232A* featuring the throttle levers for its twin *BMW 801A* radial piston engines.

The port side upper instrument panel in the *Arado Ar 232A* featuring artificial horizon and compass.

Port side metal pilot's seat in the *Arado Ar 232A*.

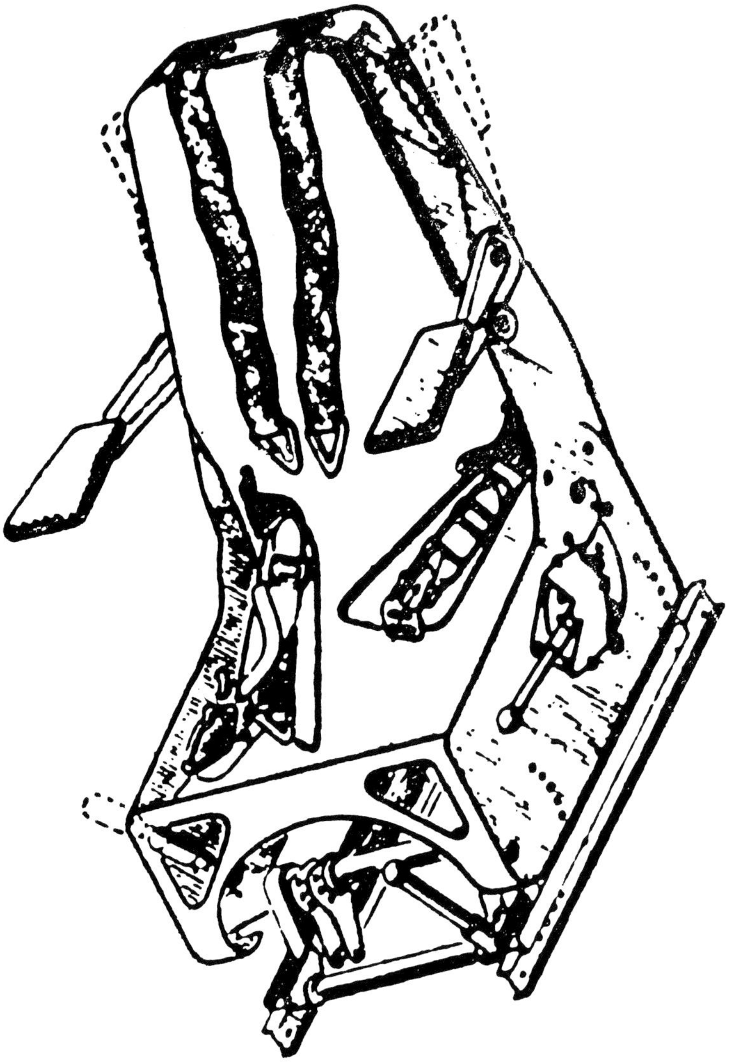

A drawing of the metal pilot's seat in the *Arado Ar 232A*.

An illustration from *Arado Flugzeugbau* of the flight control column found in the cockpit of an *Arado Ar 232A*

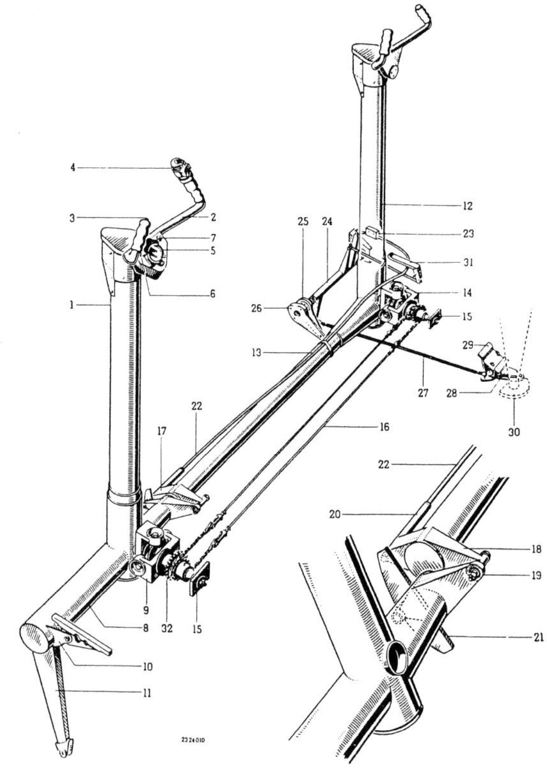

1 Steuersäule für Führer
2 Handrad
3 Druckknopf für Bremsschirm-Entreffung
4 Richtungsgeber für Kurssteuerung
5 Borduhr
6 Druckknopf für Borduhrbeleuchtung
7 Druckknopf für Funkgerät
8 Steuerwellenteil der Führersteuersäule
9 Kardangelenklager
10 Lagerhebel
11 Steuerwellenhebel für Höhensteuerung
12 Steuersäule mit Handrad für Bordwart
13 Steuerwellenteil
14 Kardangelenklager
15 Lagerplatte an Spant 3
16 Steuerzug-Quersteuerung
17 Steuerwellen-Kupplung, verriegelt
18 Steuerwellen-Kupplung, entriegelt
19 Drehpunkt der Kupplung
20 Riegelbolzenführung
21 Riegelbolzen-Führungsblech
22 Bowdenzug
23 Bowdenzugführung
24 Hebelwelle
25 Sperrhebel
26 Anschlag
27 Stoßstange
28 Umlenkhebel mit Rolle
29 Lagerbock
30 Nockenscheibe unten am Bordwartsitz
31 Bedienhebel für Steuerwellen-Kupplun
32 Kettenrad für Quersteuerantrieb

Steuersäulen

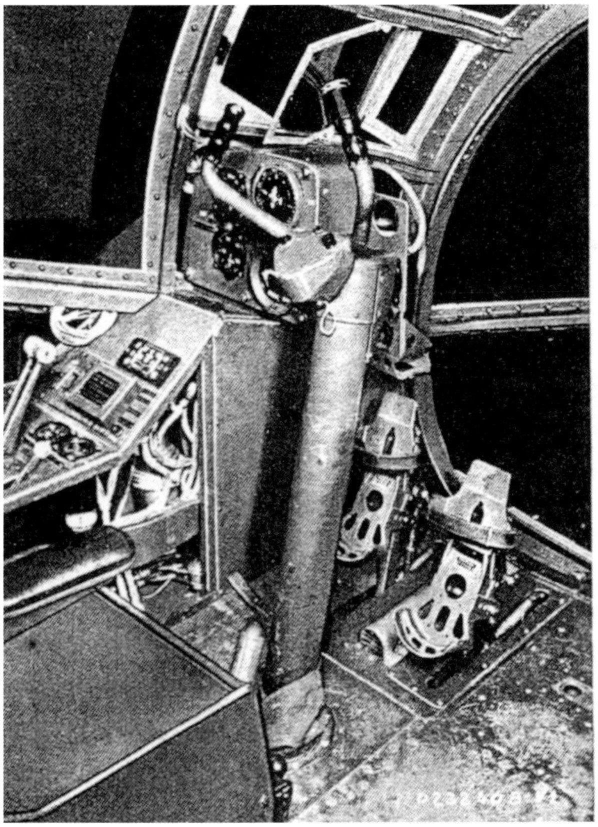

Left photo: port side pilot's control column, foot pedals, and instrument panel. Right photo: starboard side pilot's control column, foot pedals, and instrument panel found in an *Arado Ar 232A*.

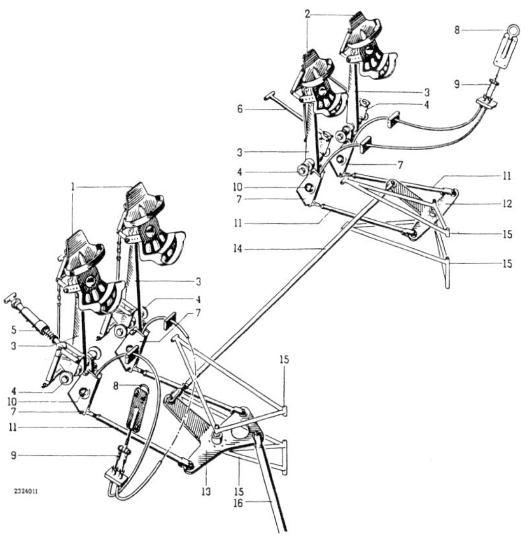

1 Fußplatte mit Druckgebergestänge der Bremsanlage für Führersteuerung
2 Fußplatte mit Gestänge für Bordwartsteuerung
3 Fußhebel für Fußplatte
4 Fußhebelachse mit Winkelhebel
5 Druckgeber zur Bremsanlage
6 Rohrstrebe am Bremsgestänge
7 Stützblech mit Verstellrasten
8 Zugring an linke und rechte Bedienbank für Fußhebelverstellung
9 Verstellzüge mit Führungen zur Fußhebelverstellung
10 Riegelbolzen an Verstellzüge
11 Stoßstange zum Umlenkhebel
12 Dreifach-Umlenkhebel
13 Vierfach-Umlenkhebel
14 Stoßstange zwischen den Umlenkhebeln
15 Lagerbock für Umlenkhebel
16 Stoßstange zum Übertragungsgestänge

Seitensteuer- und Bremspedale

An illustration from *Arado Flugzeugbau* featuring the pilot operated foot pedals for elevator controls and connecting linkage found in the *Arado Ar 232A*.

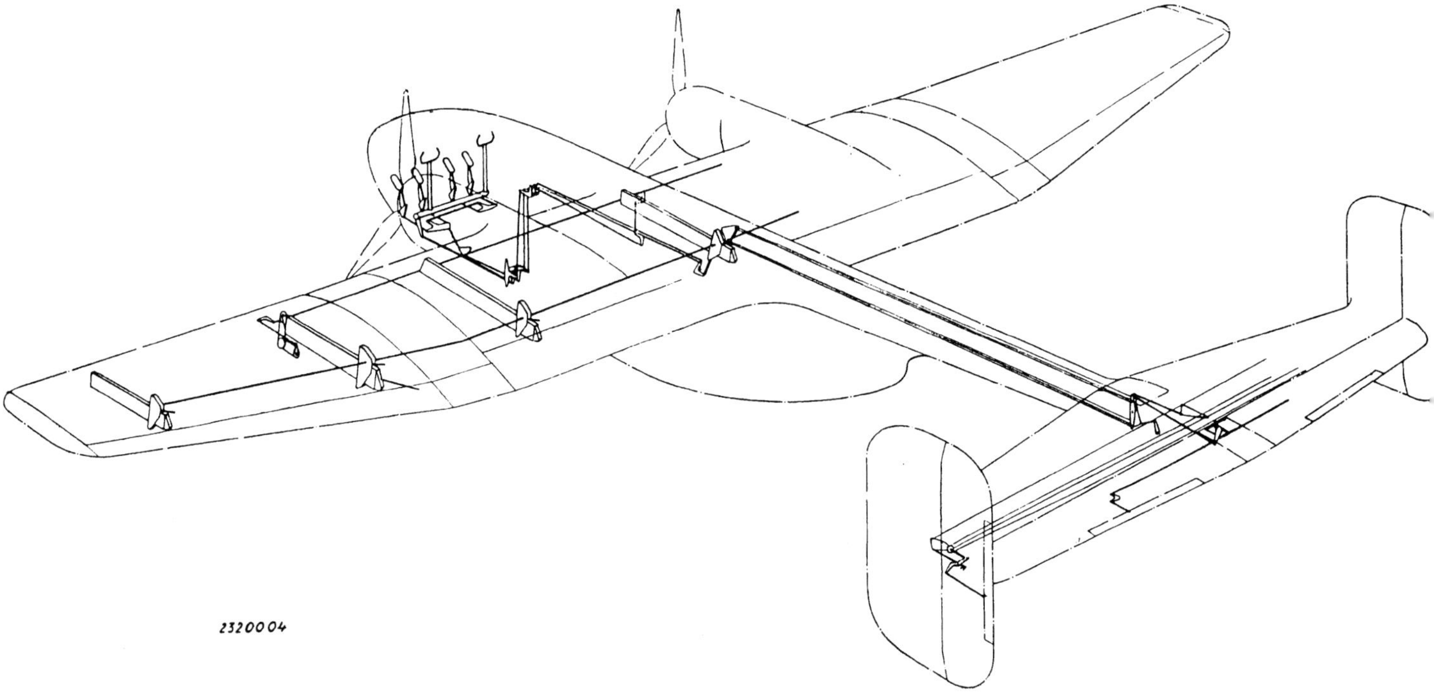

Gesamtübersicht des Steuerwerkes

An illustration from *Arado Flugzeugbau* of the flight control linkage found in the *Arado Ar 232A* between the pilot's control column and the control surfaces in the wing and tail.

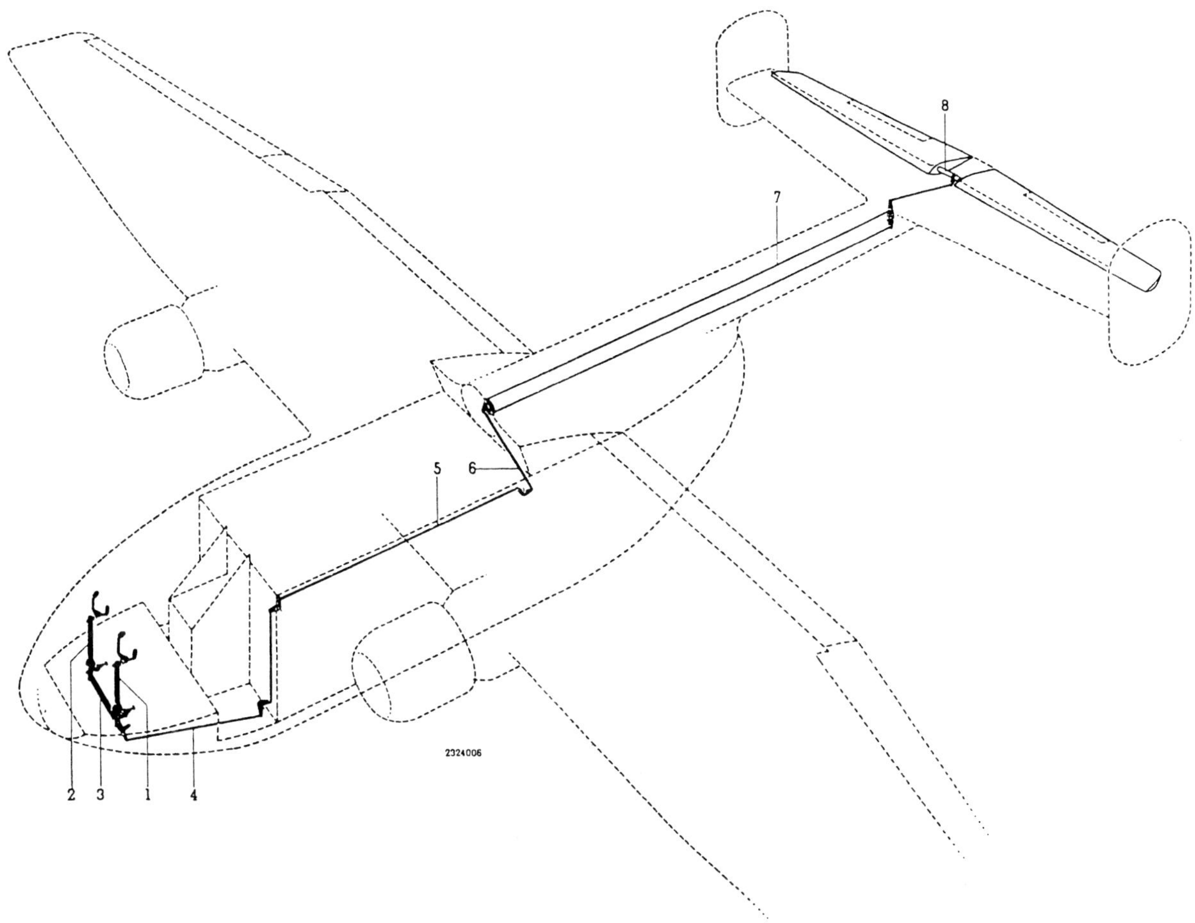

1 Steuersäule für Führer
2 Steuersäule für Bordwart
3 Steuerwelle
4 Höhensteuergestänge im Führerraum
5 Höhensteuergestänge im Laderaum
6 Höhensteuergestänge im Flügelmittelteil
7 Höhensteuergestänge in der Höhenflosse
8 Kupplungswelle mit Antriebshebel

Höhensteuerung

Ilustration from *Arado Flugzeugbau* featuring the control linkage between the control column in the cockpit and the elevators in the tail assembly on an *Arado Ar 232A*.

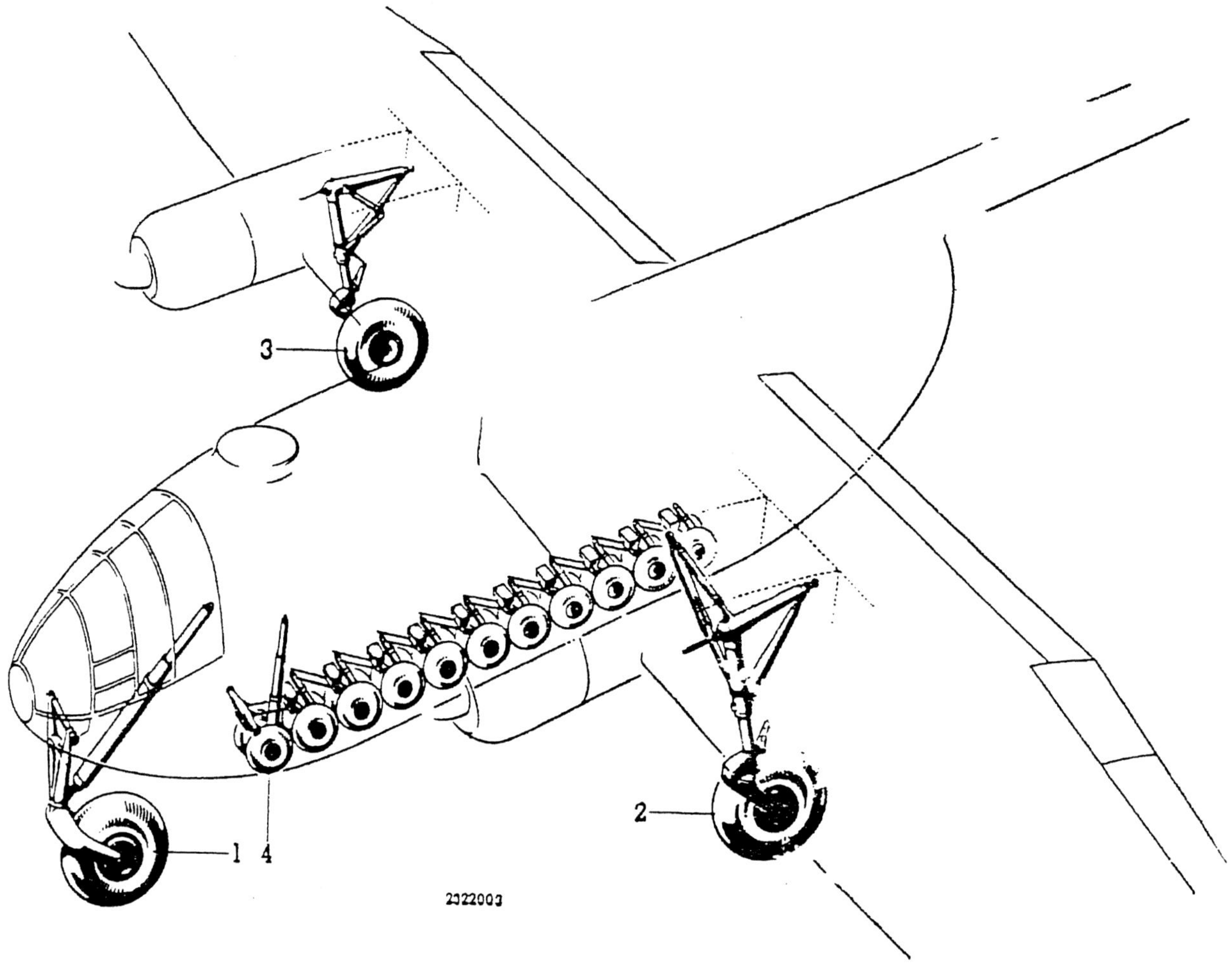

Übersicht über das Fahrwerk

An illustration from *Arado Flugzeugbau* featuring the entire undercarriage found on an *Arado Ar 232A* and *Ar 232B* combat zone transport, which includes its tricycle landing gear and 11 rows of 22 pneumatic tires located beneath the fuseláge.

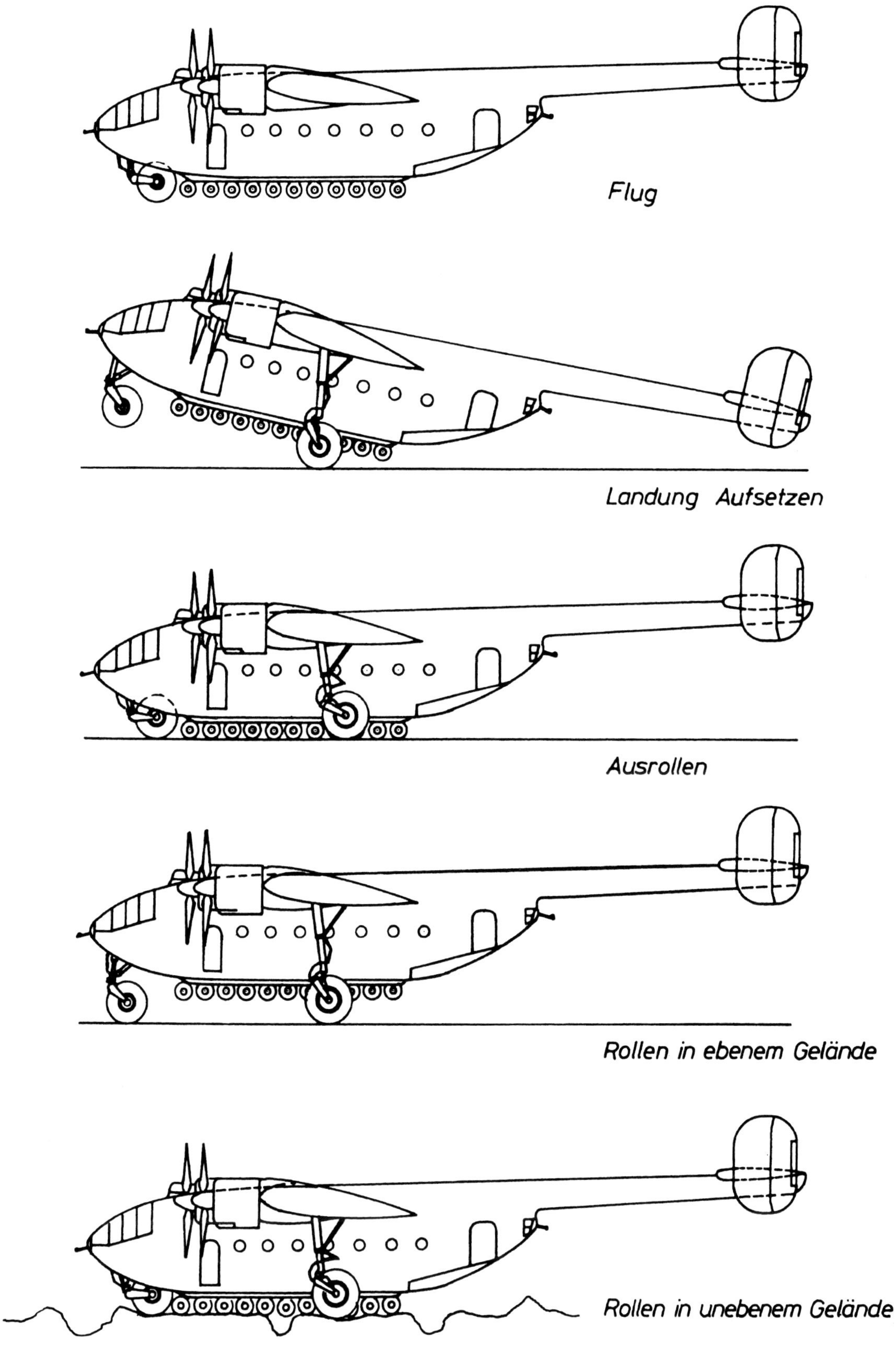

An illustration from *Arado Flugzeugbau* featuring how its undercarriage responds to variations in landing field surfaces during landing and takeoff. This illustration features the four motored *Arado Ar 232B*.

An *Arado Ar 232A* seen shortly after takeoff as it passes over the cameraman, and giving a good view of its undercarriage. Scale model and photographed by *Günter Sengfelder.*

A side view of an *Arado Ar 232A* and its 11 rows of 22 tires down on the tarmac. Scale model and photographed by *Günter Sengfelder.*

A port side nose ground level view of an *Arado Ar 232A* featuring is port side main wheel and oleo structure. Scale model and photographed by *Günter Sengfelder.*

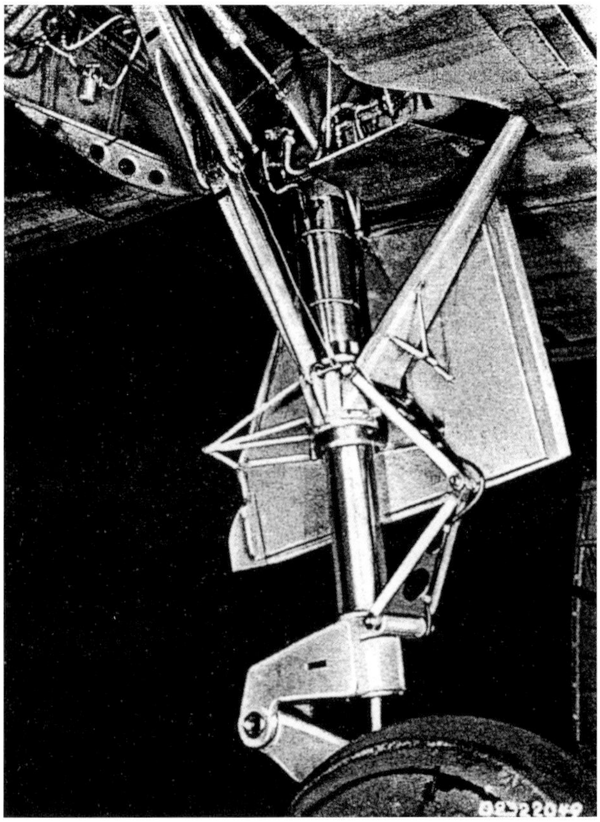

The port side main landing wheel and oleo structure of an *Arado Ar 232A* and seen from behind the wheel.

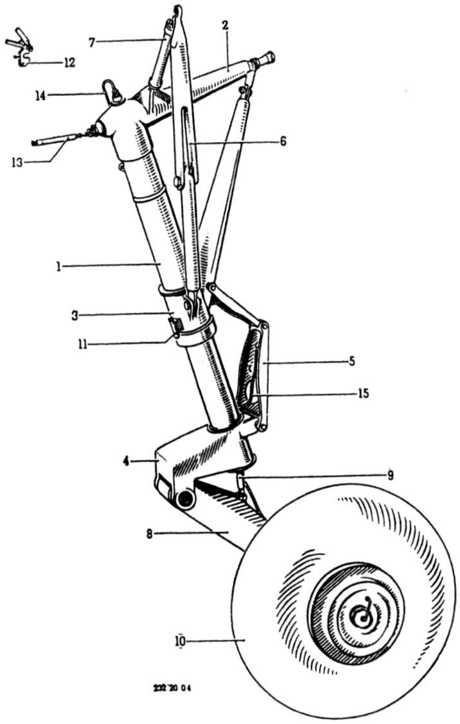

1 KPZ-Ringfederbein
2 Schwenkachse
3 Schwenkachsenmuffe mit Strebe
4 Anschlußkopf
5 Lenkhebel
6 Knickstrebe
7 Hydraulik-Arbeitszylinder
8 Schwenkarm
9 Stoßstange
10 Laufrad
11 Rolle für Fahrgestellaufhängung
12 Aufhängevorrichtung
13 Stützstrebe zur Schwenkachse
14 Drucköleitung für KPZ-Ringfederbein
15 Laufrad-Bremsleitung

Seitliches Fahrgestell rechts

An illustration from *Arado Flugzeugbau* of the port side main landing gear on an *Arado Ar 232A* as seen from the inside.

A nose-on view of the starboard side main landing gear on an *Arado Ar 232A*. Scale model and photographed by *Günter Sengfelder.*

A view inside the wing of the starboard side main landing gear on an *Arado Ar 232A*

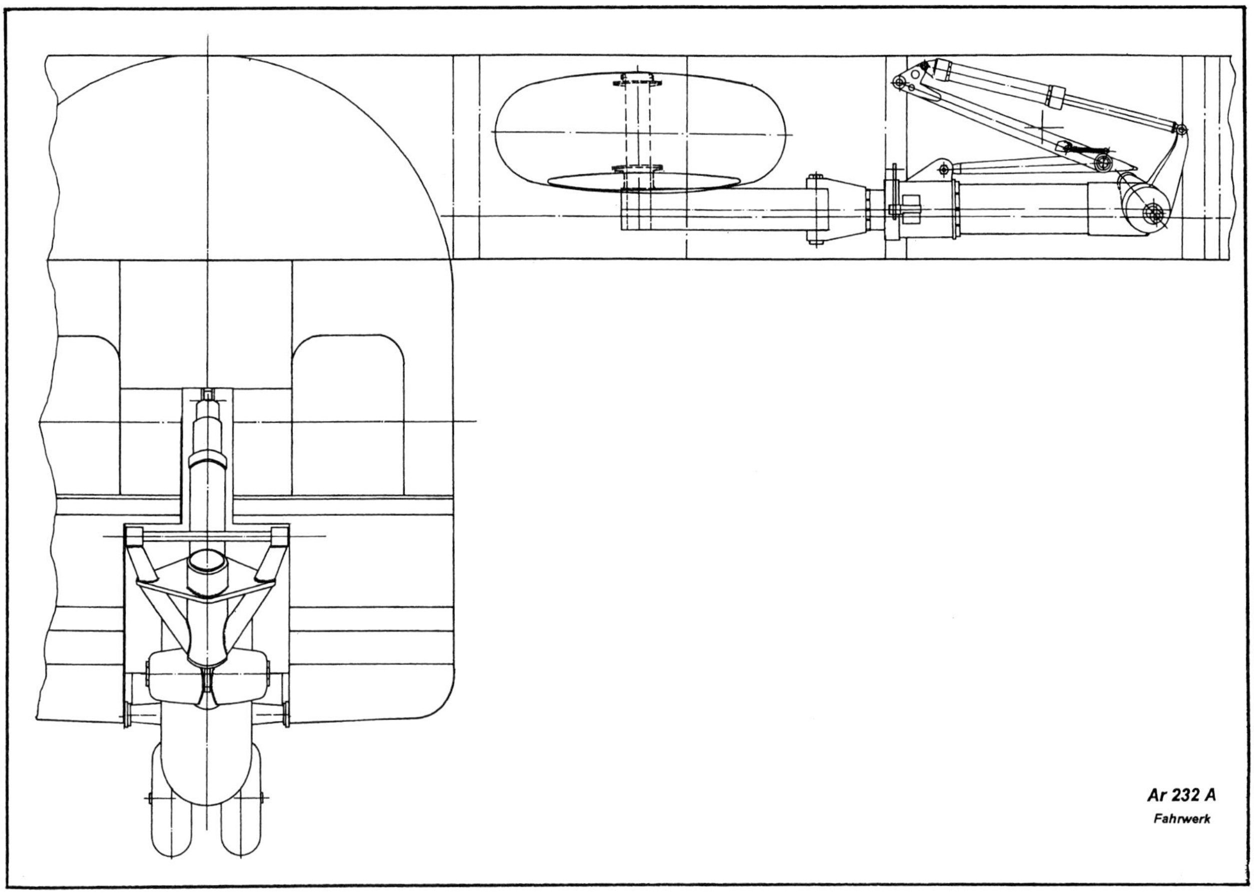

An illustration featuring the port side main landing gear and wheel in its retracted position, as well as the nose wheel. Drawing by *Günter Sengfelder.*

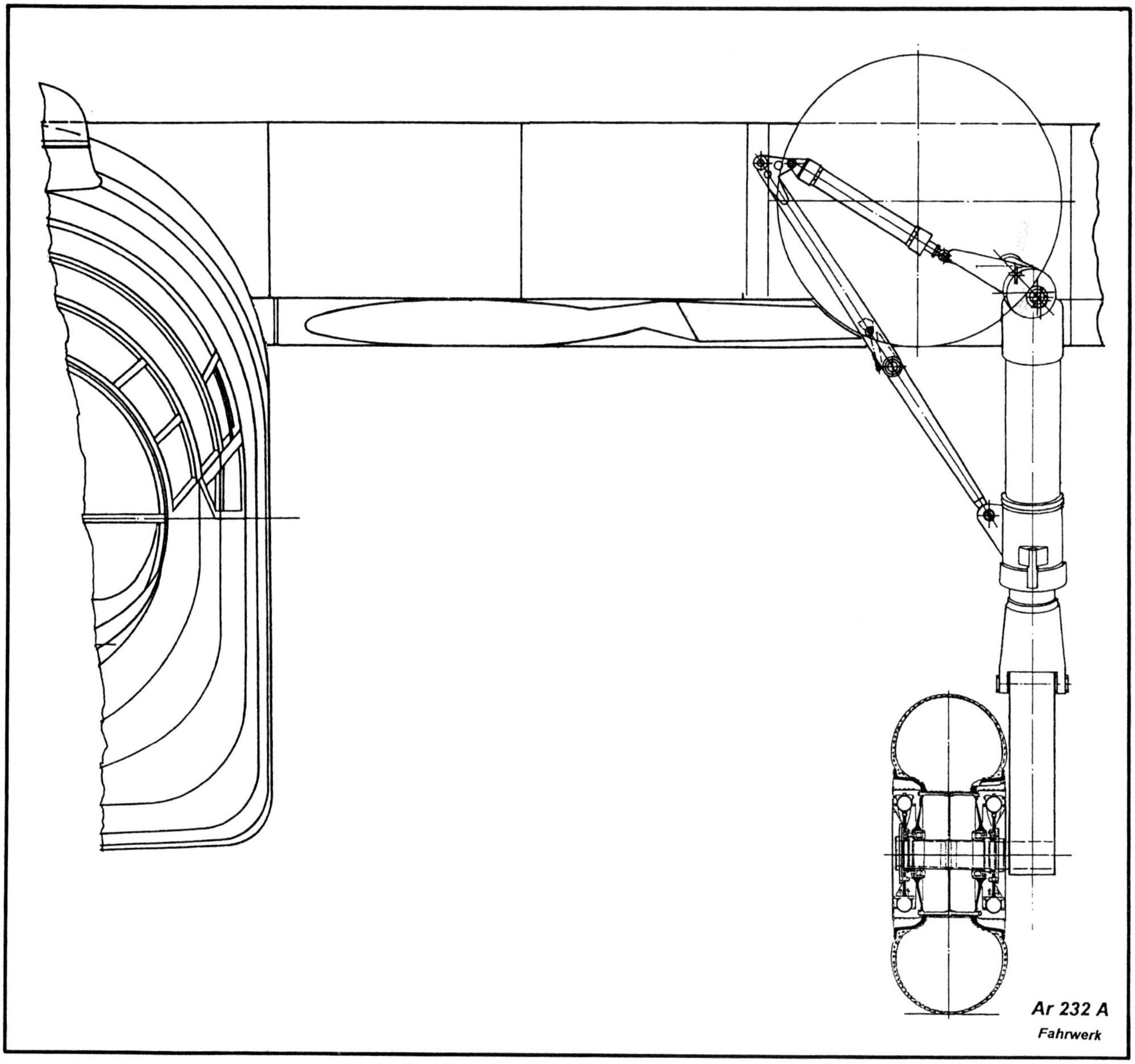

An illustration featuring the port side main landing gear fully extended. Drawing by *Günter Sengfelder.*

A nose-on view of an *Arado Ar 232A* featuring its port side main landing gear. Scale model and photographed by *Günter Sengfelder.*

A starboard side view of an *Arado Ar 232A* as seen from below with its main landing gear and wheel fully retracted. Scale model and photographed by *Günter Sengfelder.*

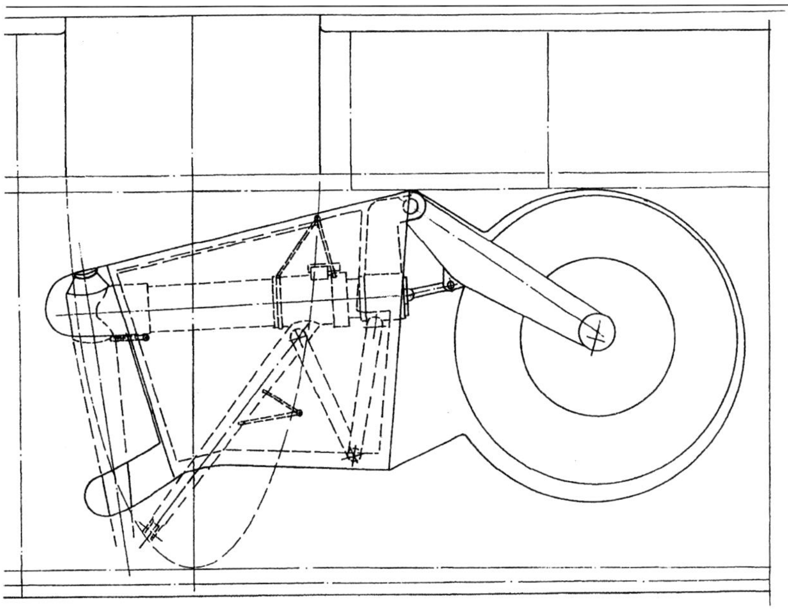

An illustration featuring the position of a fully retracted starboard side main landing gear and wheel as viewed from beneath. Drawing by *Günter Sengfelder.*

An *Arado Ar 232A* viewed from beneath and featuring its 11 rows of 22 tires and its port side main landing gear and wheel fully extended. Scale model and photographed by *Günter Sengfelder.*.

The same photo as seen on the opposite page, however, its port side main landing gear is shown fully retracted. Scale model and photographed by *Günter Sengfelder.*

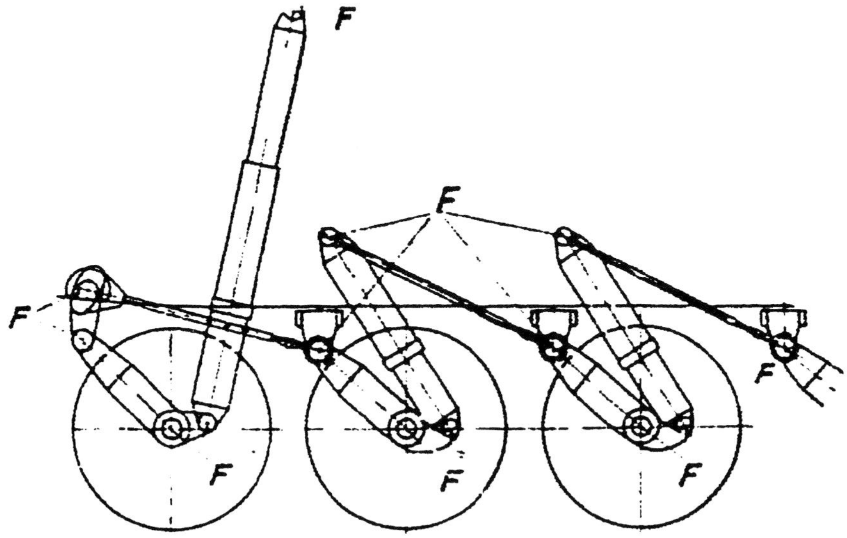

An illustration by *Arado Flugzeugbau* featuring the first 3 rows of center fuselage-mounted caterpillar-style landing wheels as found on the *Arado Ar 232A*.

An *Arado Ar 232A* seen from its starboard nose side shortly after lift off featuring a good view of its 11 rows of 22 pneumatic landing wheels/tires mounted to the underside of its fuselage. Scale model and photographed by Günter *Sengfelder.*

An *Arado Ar 232A* seen from its port side shortly after lift off and featuring a good view of its 11 rows of 22 pneumatic landing wheels/tires mounted to the underside of its fuselage. Scale model and photographed by *Günter Sengfelder.*

A photo from Arado flugzeugbau of their *Arado Ar 232A* featuring the first 3 rows of its fuselage mounted landing wheel tires as seen from the starboard side and featuring their simple single oleo struts. These fuselage-mounted wheels did not retract.

The last row of fuselage-mounted landing wheels on the *Arado Ar 232A* combat zone transporter as seen from its port rear side.

A port side view of one of the 11 rows of fuselage-mounted fixed landing wheels on an *Arado Ar 232A*.

A port side view of an *Arado Ar 232A* featuring the entry door to the forward fuselage. Notice the first four rows of fuselage-mounted landing wheels appear to be just hanging under the fuselage.

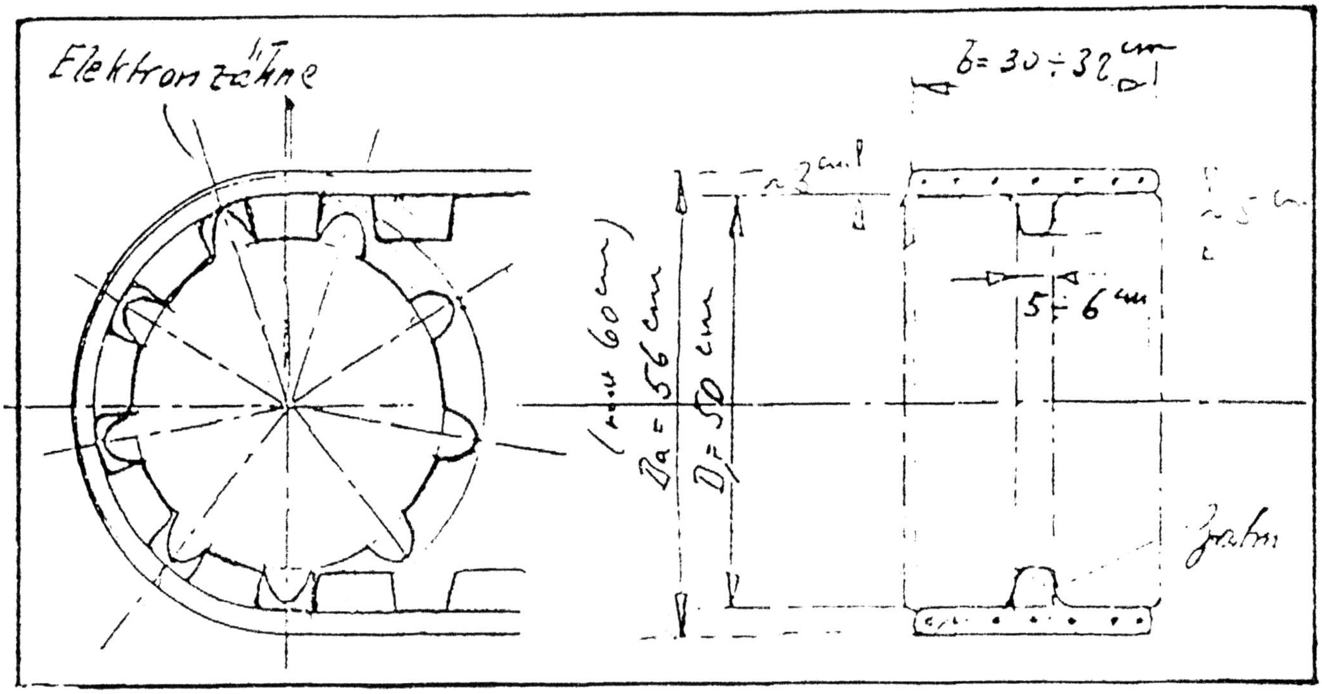

A crude drawing of the proposed caterpillar-like track intended on the 11 rows of fuselage-mounted landing wheels by Arado flugzeugbau. It is believed by *Arado Flugzeugbau* designers that this track would have allowed the *Ar 232A* to land and take off in snow more effectively.

A starboard side rear view of the tail boom and dual rudder assembly on the *Arado Ar 232A*.

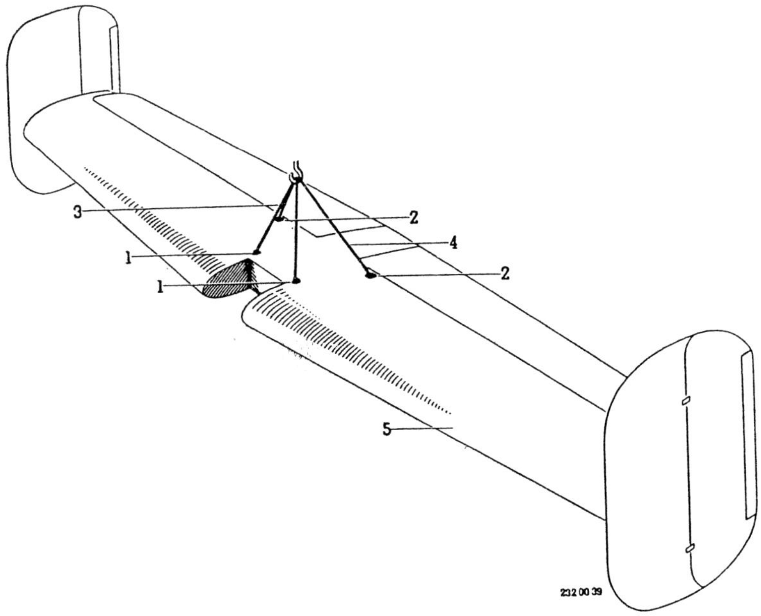

1 Augbeschläge am Vorderholm
2 Augbeschläge am Hinterholm
3 Vorderes Heißseil
4 Hinteres Heißseil
5 Heckleitwerk

An illustration from *Arado Flugzeugbau* featuring the lifting eye locations for lifting the entire tail assembly of an *Arado Ar 232A/B*.

A close up view of the tail assembly on an *Arado Ar 232A* as seen from its port side rear. Scale model and photographed by *Günter Sengfelder*.

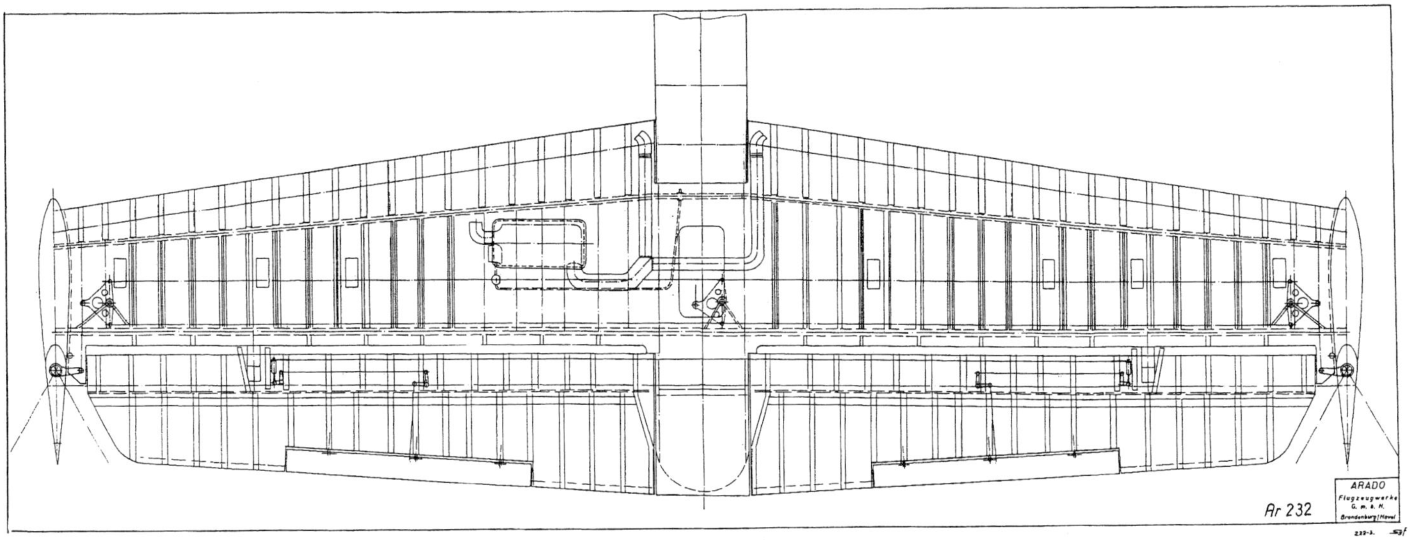

An illustration from *Arado Flugzeugbau* featuring an internal view of the tail assembly span between the dual rudders on an *Arado Ar 232A/B*.

Arado Ar 232A. Scale model and photographed by *Günter Sengfelder.*

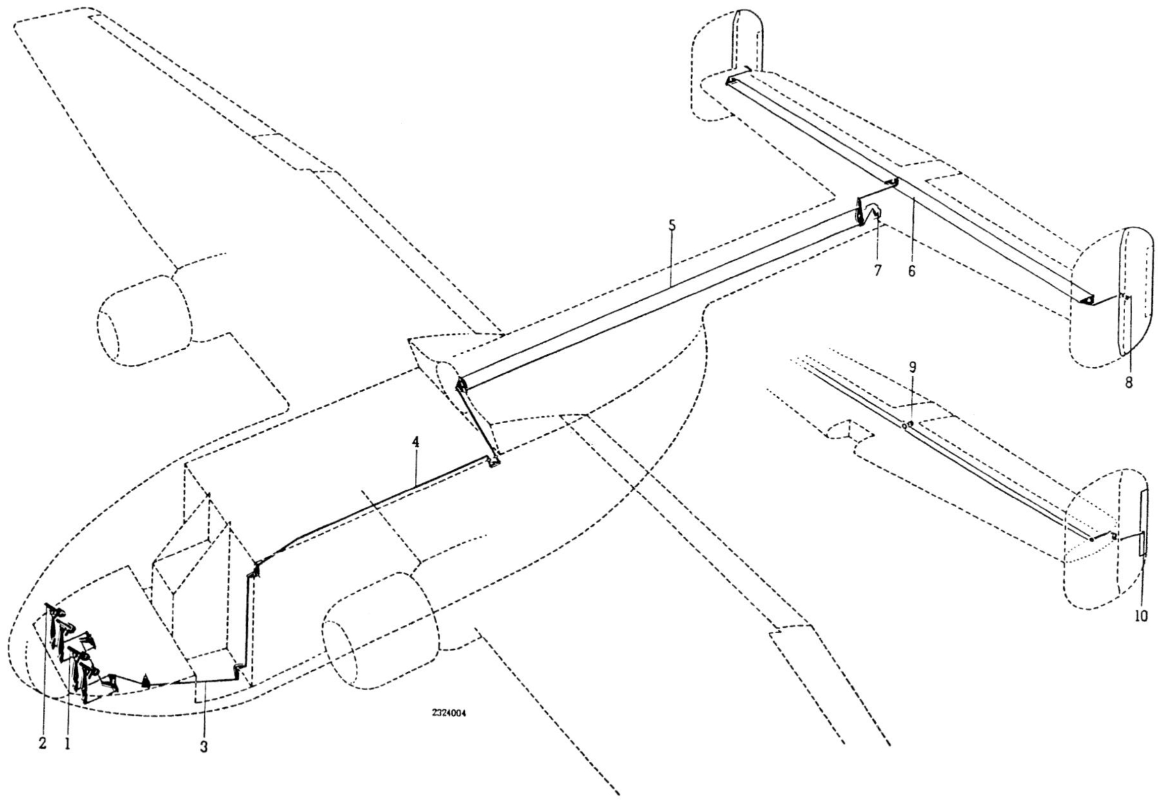

1 Seitensteuer- und Bremspedale für Führer
2 Seitensteuer- und Bremspedale für Bordwart
3 Seitensteuergestänge im Führerraum
4 Seitensteuergestänge im Laderaum
5 Seitensteuerzüge im Leitwerksträger
6 Seitensteuerzüge in der Höhenflosse
7 Rudermaschine für Kurssteuerung
8 Seitenruderhebel
9 Elt-Motor und Verstellzüge für Seitenrudertrimmung
10 Trimmruderhebel

Seitensteuerung

An illustration from *Arado Flugzeugbau* featuring the control linkage to the rudders located in the tail assembly from pilot's foot pedals in the cockpit found in an *Arado Ar 232A/B*.

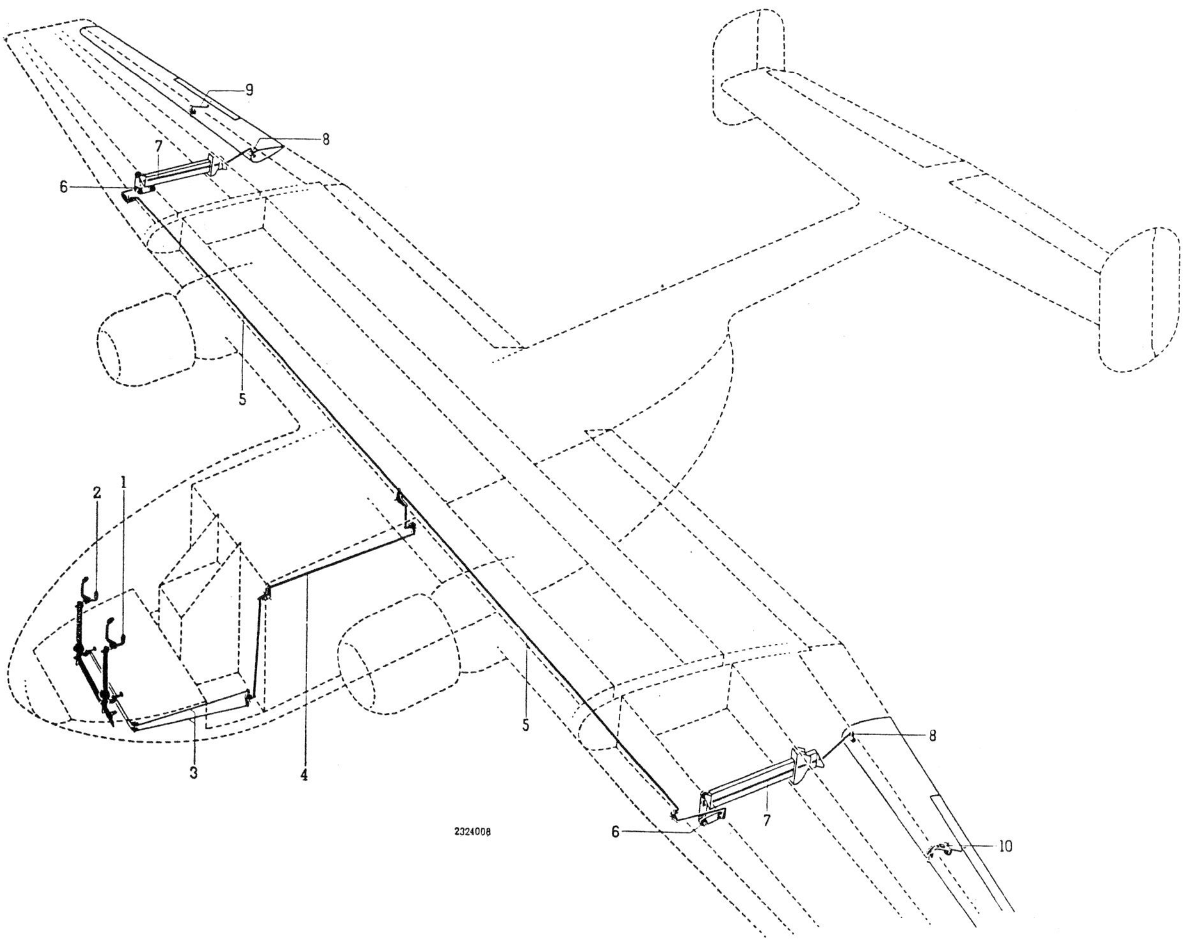

1 Handrad für Führer	6 Quersteuerumlegung
2 Handrad für Bordwart	7 Stoßstange im Landeflügel-Ausleger
3 Quersteuerzüge im Führerraum	8 Stoßstange am Querruderhebel
4 Quersteuergestänge im Laderaum	9 Stoßstange für Ausgleichsruder
5 Quersteuergestänge im Tragwerk	10 Antriebsgestänge für Trimmruder

An illustration from *Arado Flugzeugbau* featuring the control linkage to the ailerons in the trailing edges of the port and starboard wing from the control column in the cockpit found in an *Arado Ar 232A/B*.

The port underside wing of an *Arado Ar 232A* featuring its outboard aileron and aileron trim tab. Scale model and photographed by *Günter Sengfelder.*

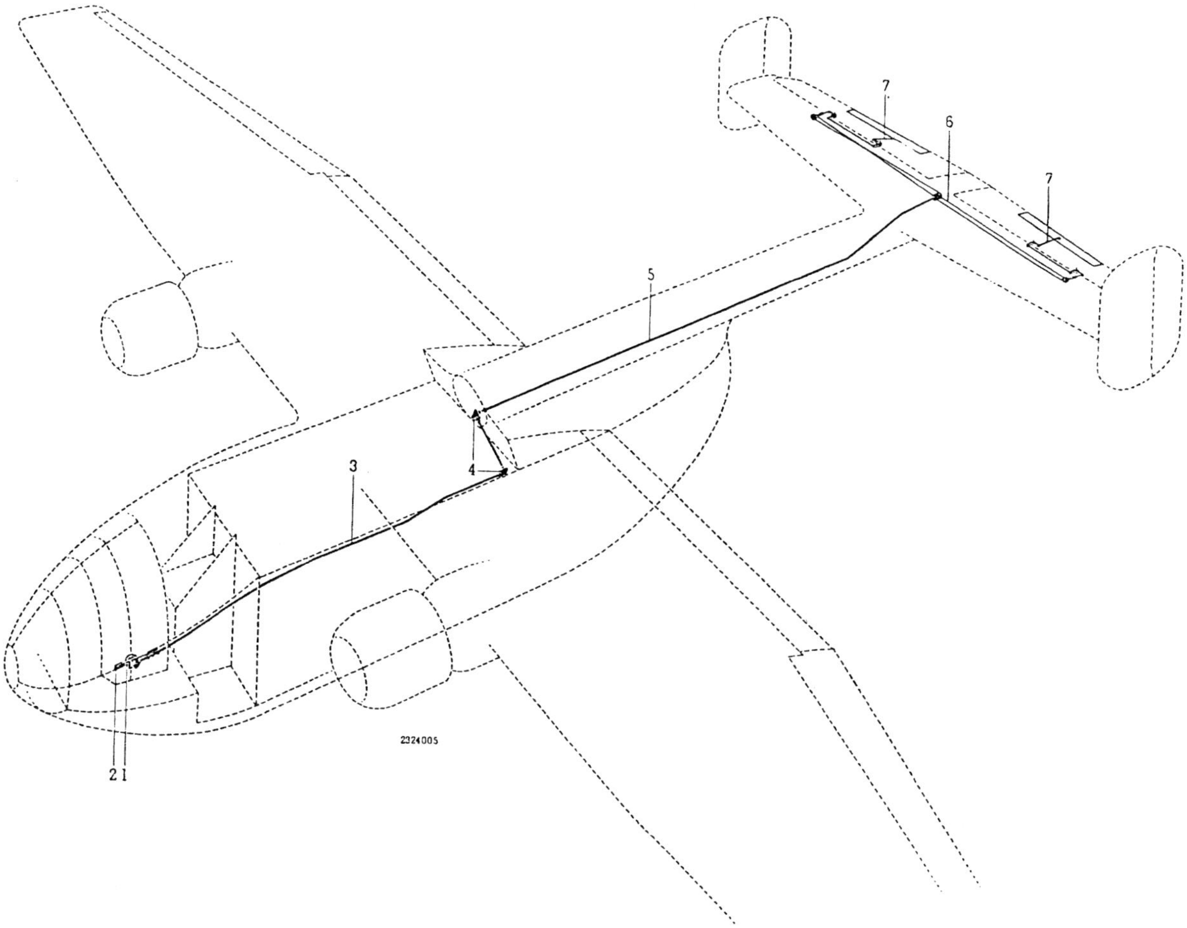

1 Handrad für Höhentrimmung
2 Anzeigegerät für Höhentrimmung
3 Gelenkwellen im Rumpf
4 Winkeltriebe
5 Gelenkwellen im Leitwerksträger
6 Höhentrimmruderzüge im Leitwerksträger
7 Stoßstange für Höhentrimmruder

Höhentrimmung

An illustration from *Arado Flugzeugbau* featuring the control linkage between the tail assembly's elevator trim tab and the cockpit of an *Arado Ar 232A/B*.

The tail assembly of *Arado Ar 232A-01* featuring the elevator trim tabs on the trailing edge of the elevators and seen from its starboard rear side.

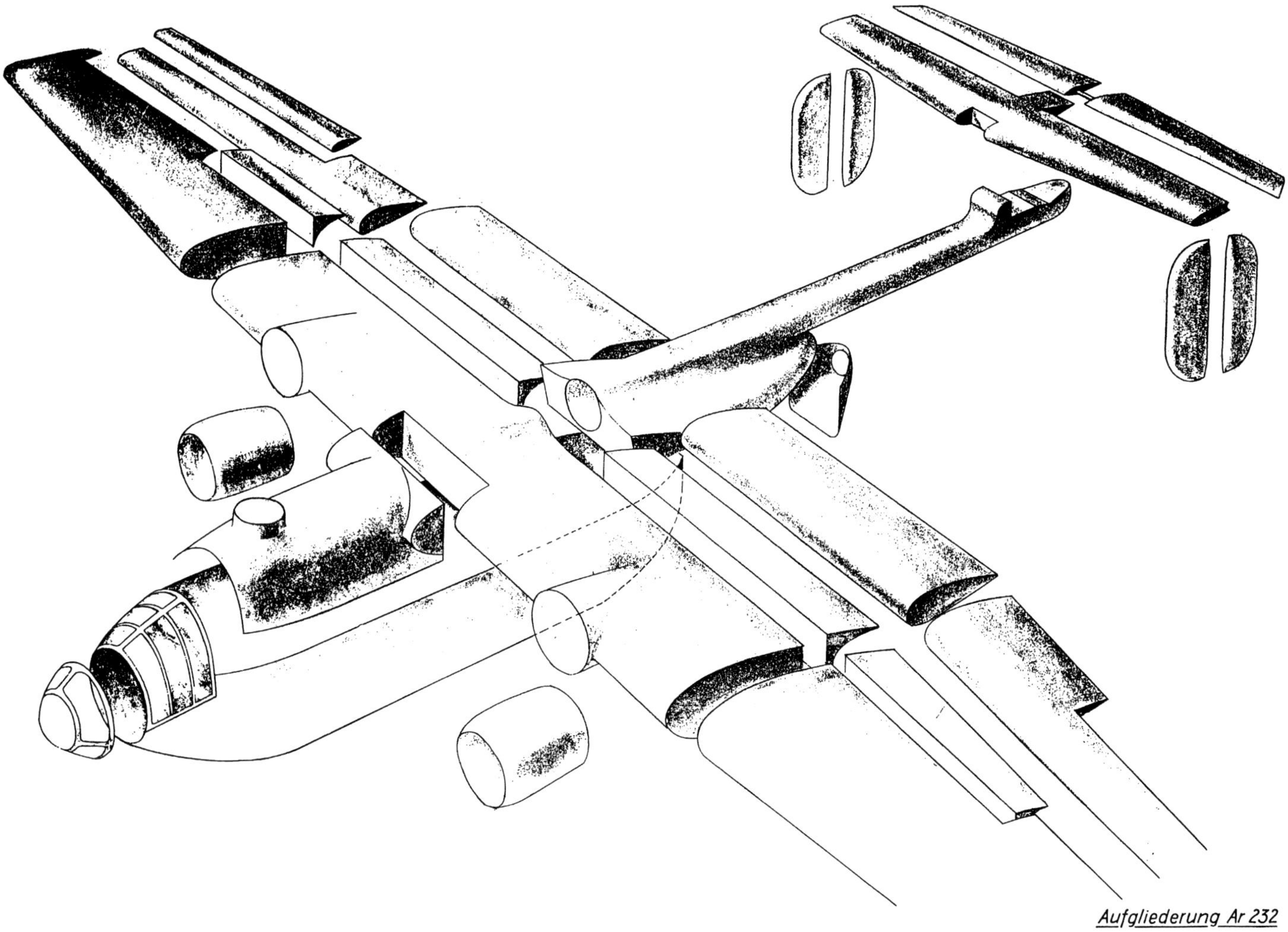

An illustration from *Arado Flugzeugbau* featuring the several component sections of the *Arado Ar 232A*.

Ar 232 A-O
Flugzeug-Handbuch

Allgemeine Angaben

O 17

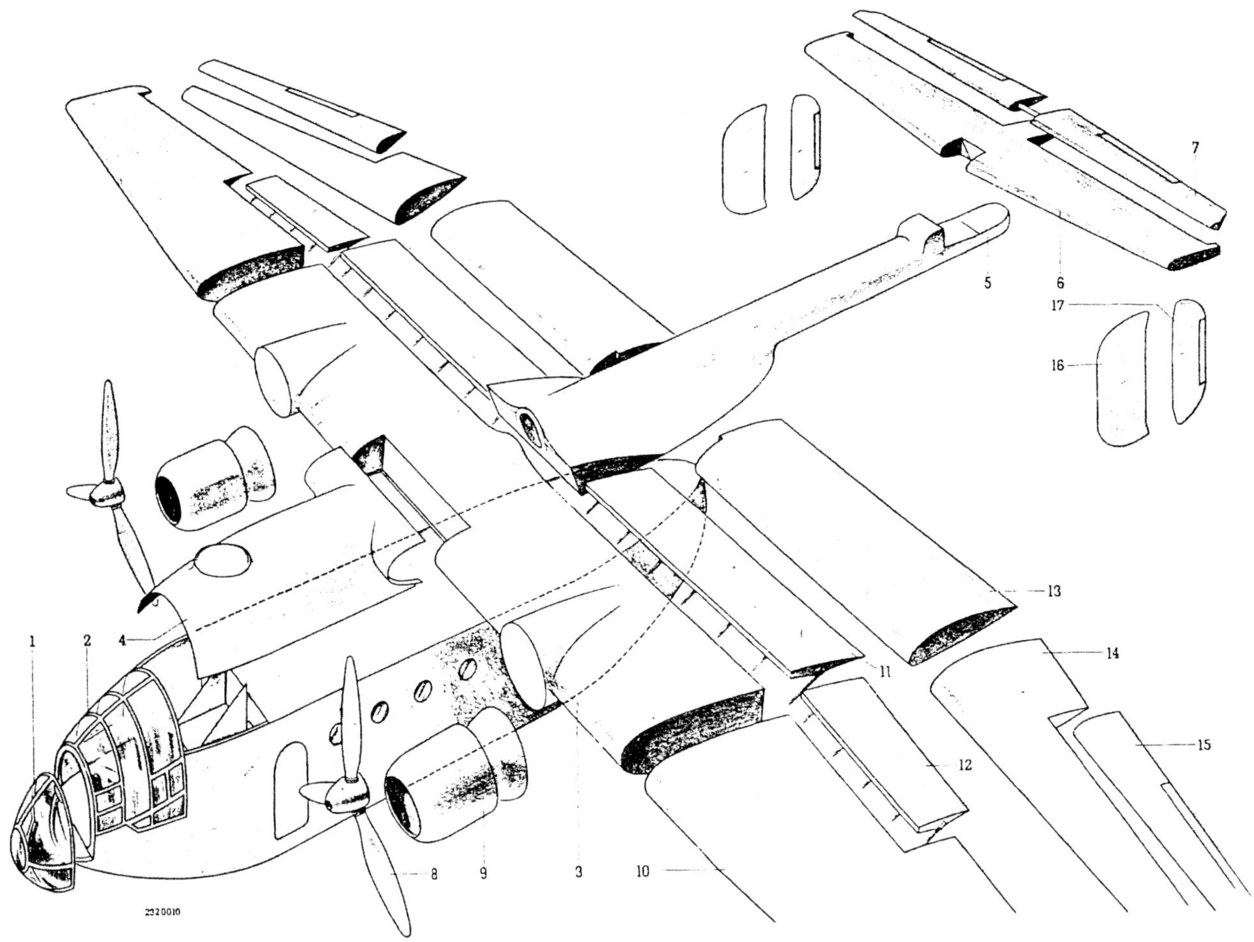

1 Rumpfbug
2 Rumpf (Lastenträger)
3 Flügelmittelteil
4 Rumpfoberteil
5 Leitwerksträger
6 Höhenflosse
7 Höhenruder mit Ausgleichsruder
8 VDM-Verstelluftschraube
9 Triebwerk
10 Außenflügel
11 Düsenkasten am Flügelmittelteil
12 Düsenkasten am Außenflügel
13 Landeflügel am Flügelmittelteil
14 Landeflügel am Außenflügel
15 Querruder mit Ausgleichsruder
16 Seitenflosse
17 Seitenruder mit Ausgleichsruder

Großbaugruppen des Flugzeugmusters

An illustration from *Arado Flugzeugbau* identifying the component sections comprising the *Arado Ar 232A* combat zone transporter.

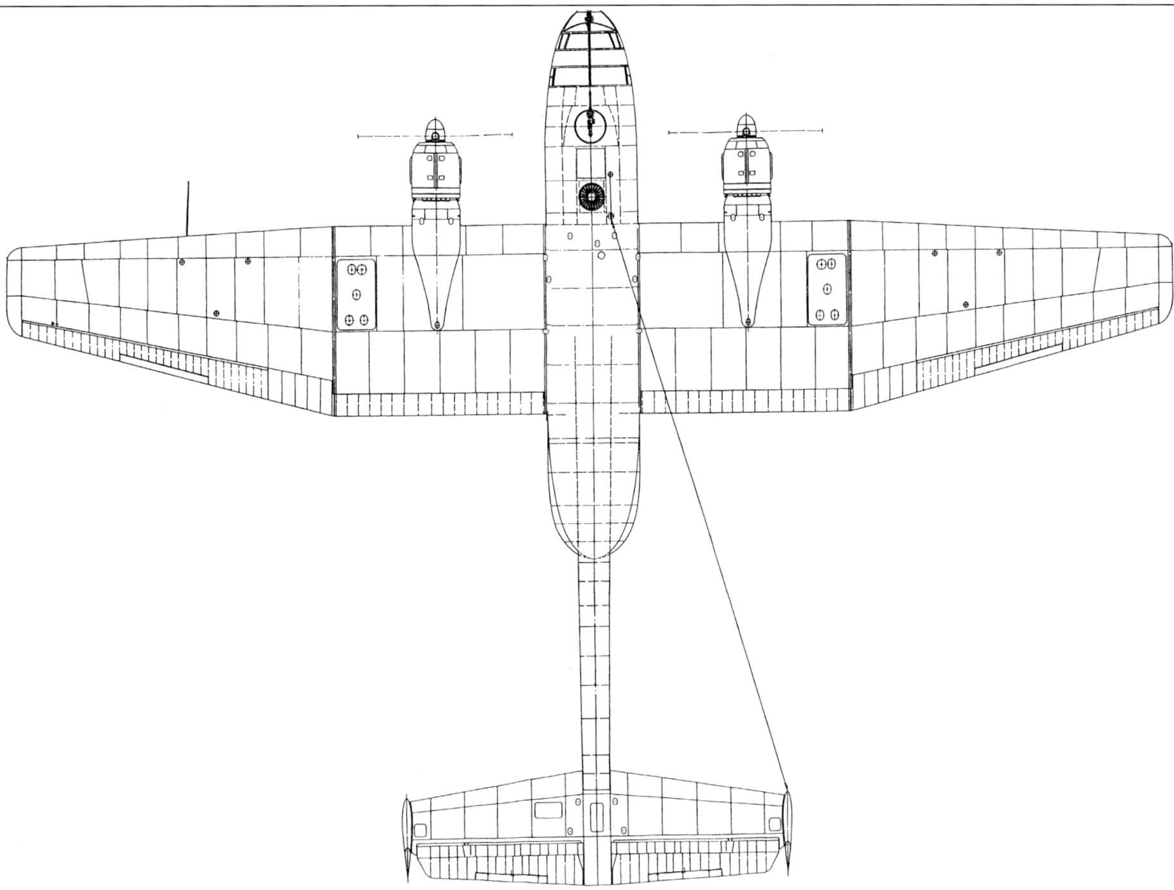

An illustration featuring the overall planform of the *Arado Ar 232A*. Drawing by *Günter Sengfelder.*

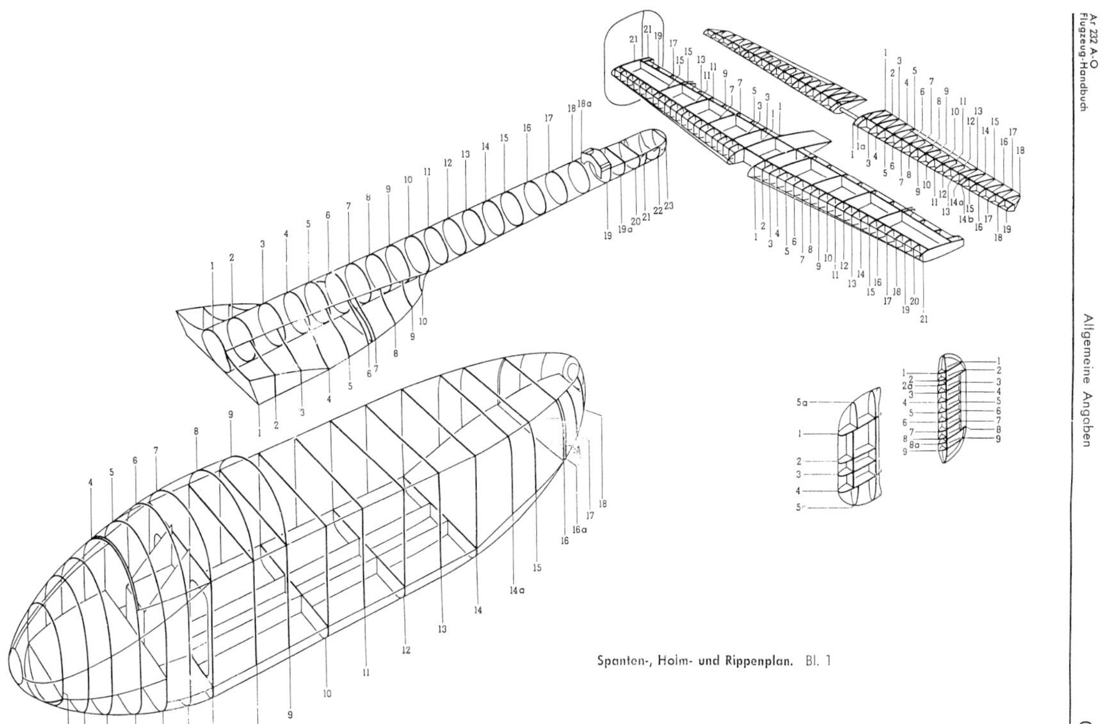

A see-through illustration from *Arado Flugzeugbau* featuring sectional cut away drawings of the fuselage, tail boom, and tail assembly of an *Arado Ar 232A/B* combat zone transporter.

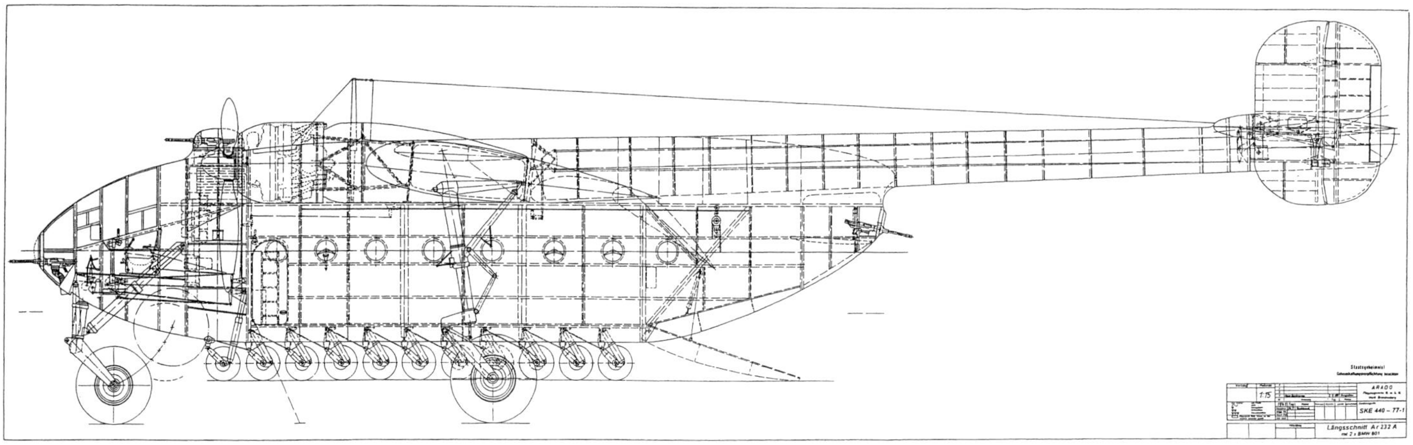

A general arrangement illustration from *Arado Flugzeugbau* featuring the port side of their *Arado Ar 232A* combat zone transporter.

A fully skinned port side view of an *Arado Ar 232A*. Compare this to the see-through illustration above. Scale model and photographed by *Günter Sengfelder.*

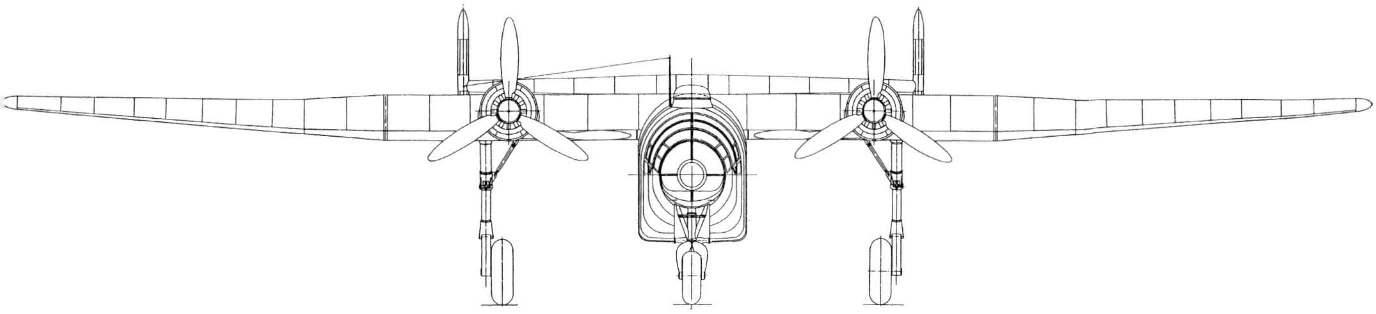

An illustration featuring nose-on ground level view of the *Arado Ar 232A*. Drawing by *Günter Sengfelder.*

A ground level nose-on view of the *Arado Ar 232A*. It features the 11 rows of caterpillar-type fuselage mounted wheels down on the tarmac. Scale model and photographed by *Günter Sengfelder.*

Ar 232 A-O
Flugzeug-Handbuch

Allgemeine Angaben

O 09

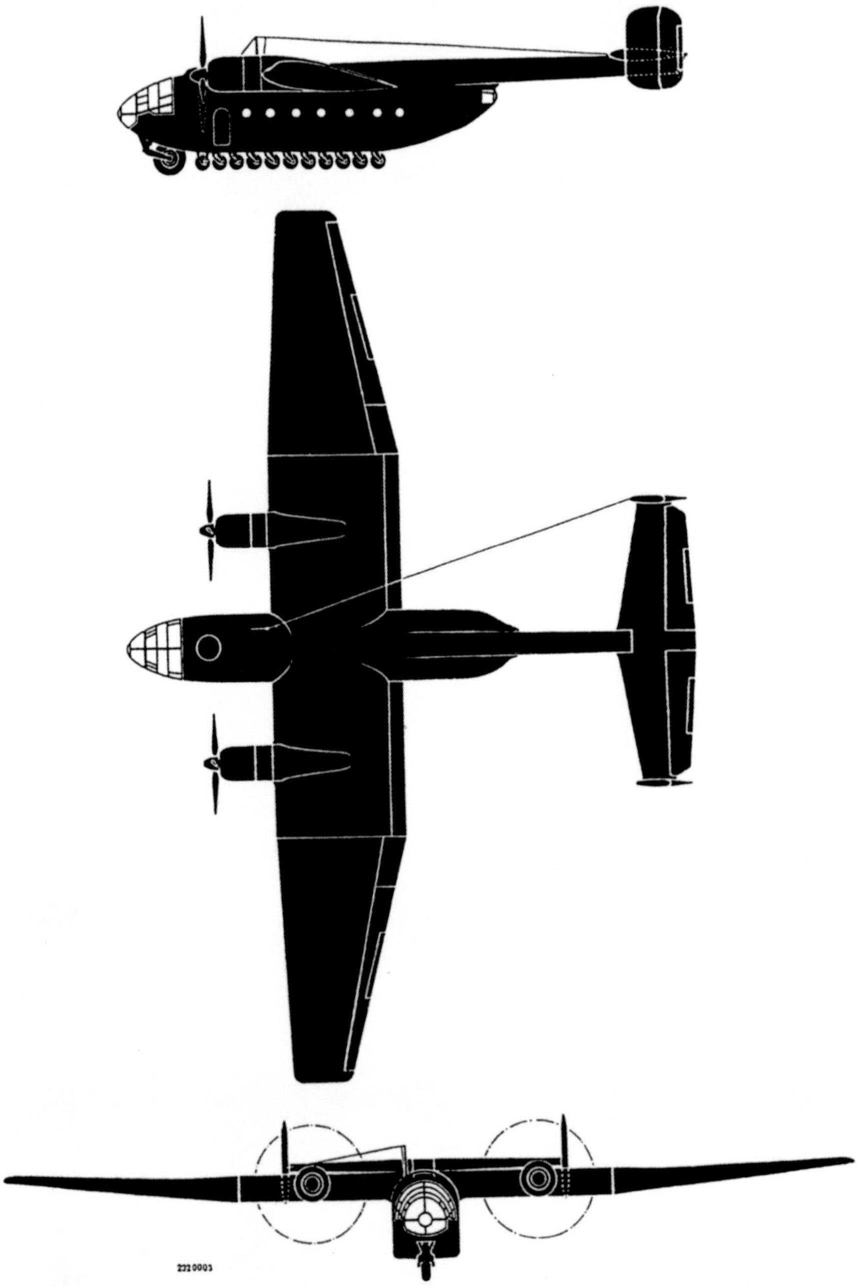

Dreischattenriß

A drawing from *Arado Flugzeugbau's* handbook featuring the *Arado Ar 232A-O* version of their combat zone transporter.

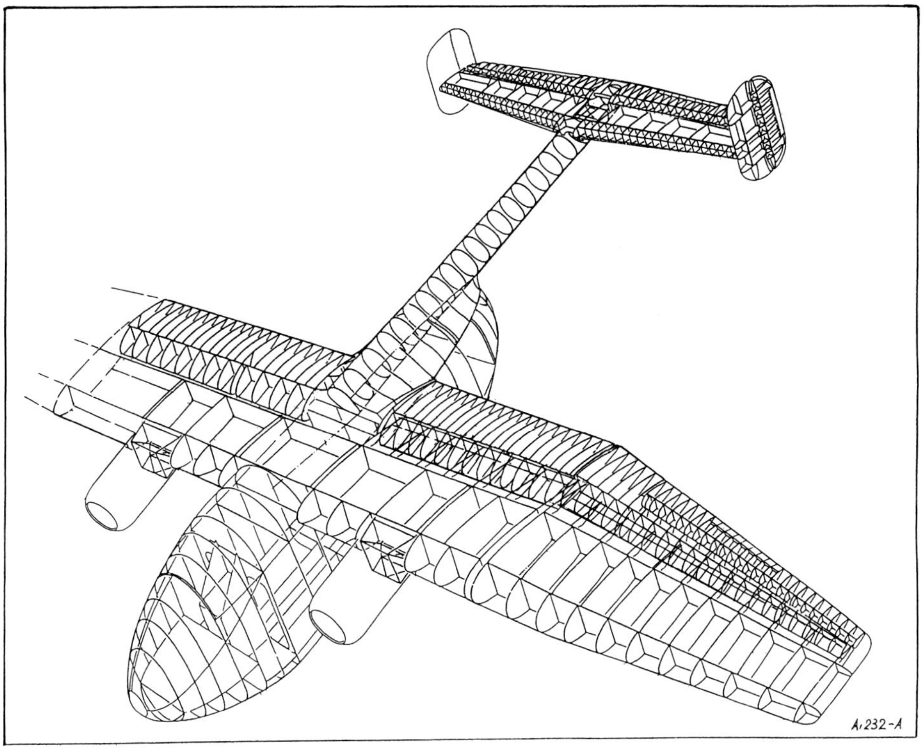

An illustration from *Arado Flugzeugbau* of their *Arado Ar 232A* and featuring fuselage bulkheads, tail boom bulkheads, wing spars, wing ribs, and tail assembly construction.

An illustration from *Arado Flugzeugbau* of their *Arado Ar 232A* featuring the structural components of the inner and outer port wing panel, landing flap, and ailerons.

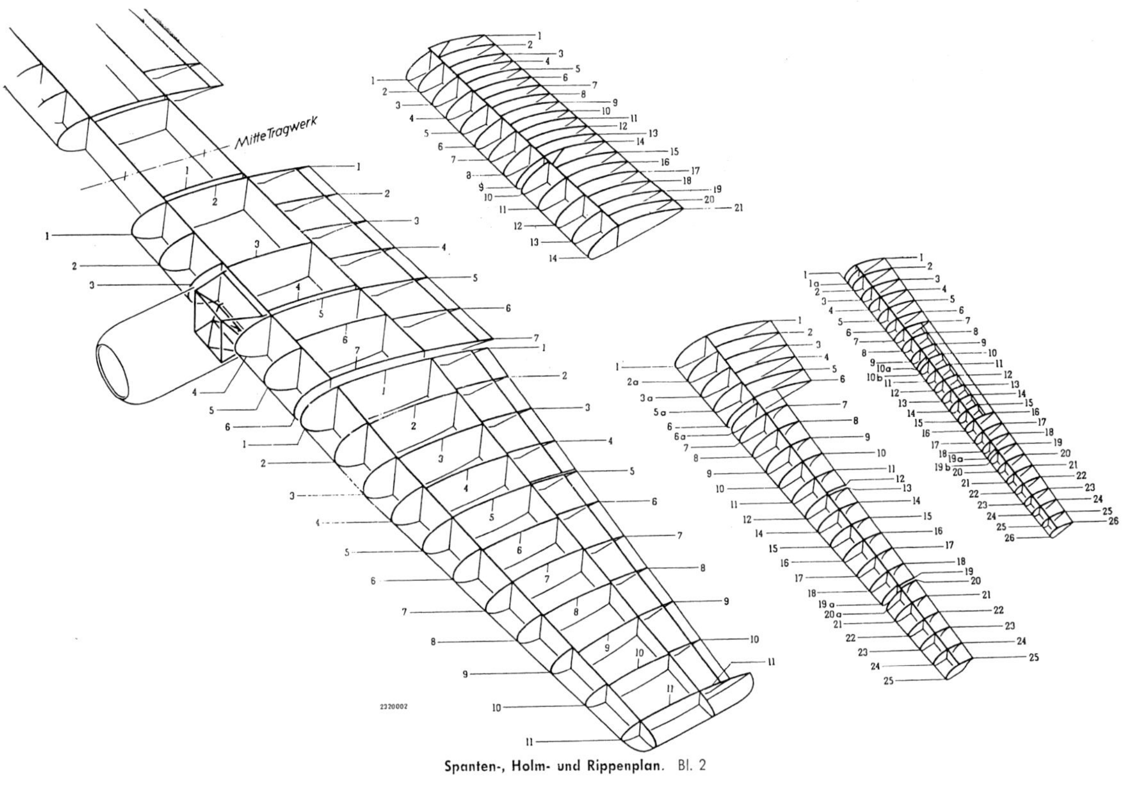

A nose-on view of the *Arado Ar 232A* with its landing flaps fully retracted. Scale model and photographed by *Günter Sengfelder.*

A nose-on view of the *Arado Ar 232A* with its landing flaps fully extended. Scale model and photographed by *Günter Sengfelder.*

A rear view of the *Arado Ar 232A* featuring its landing flaps fully extended. Scale model and photographed by *Günter Sengfelder.*

An overhead view of an *Arado Ar 232A* as seen from its rear with its landing flaps fully extended. Scale model and photographed by *Günter Sengfelder.*

A ground level port side front view of an *Arado Ar 232* with its variable pitch 14 foot [4.3 meter] diameter *VDM* propellers. Scale model and photographed by *Günter Sengfelder.*

The port side *BMW 801A* radial piston of the *Arado Ar 232A V1* prototype.

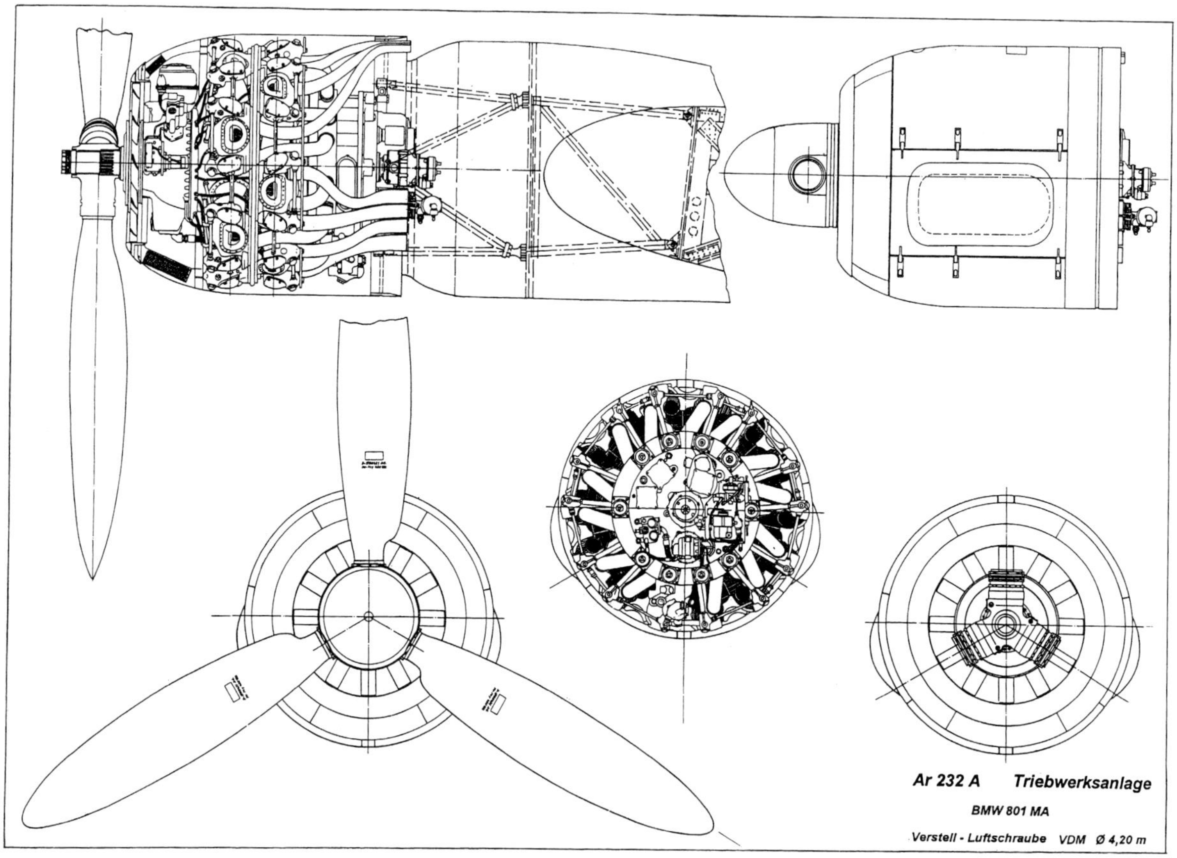

An illustration from *BMW* featuring their *BMW 801 MA* of the type placed in the *Arado Ar 232A* with its cowling open and closed.

Motoranlage BMW 801 MA u. BMW 801 ML

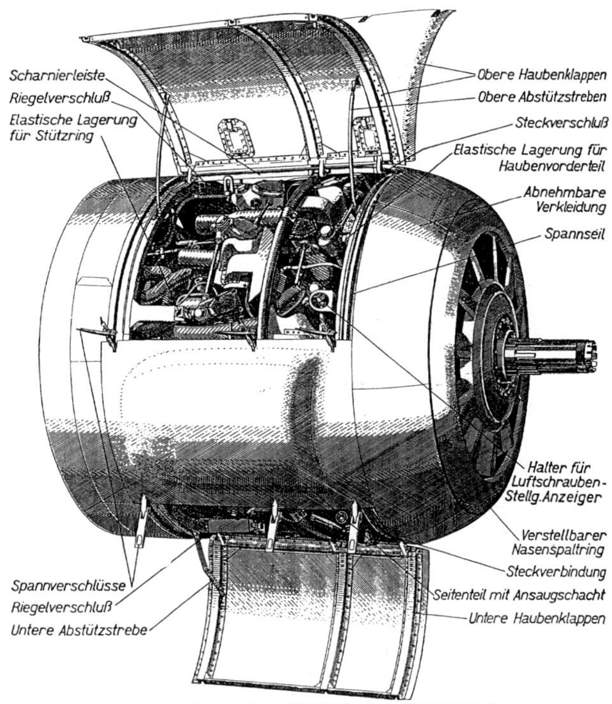

Motoranlage BMW 801 MA und BMW 801 ML mit geöffneten Haubenklappen

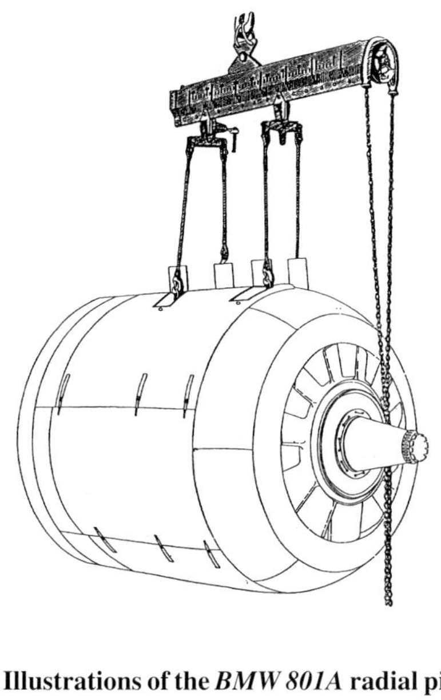

Illustrations of the *BMW 801A* radial piston engine of the type installed on the *Arado Ar 232A V1* prototype.

A port side *BMW 801A* radial piston engine with its inner engine cowling in the up position showing the engine's details.

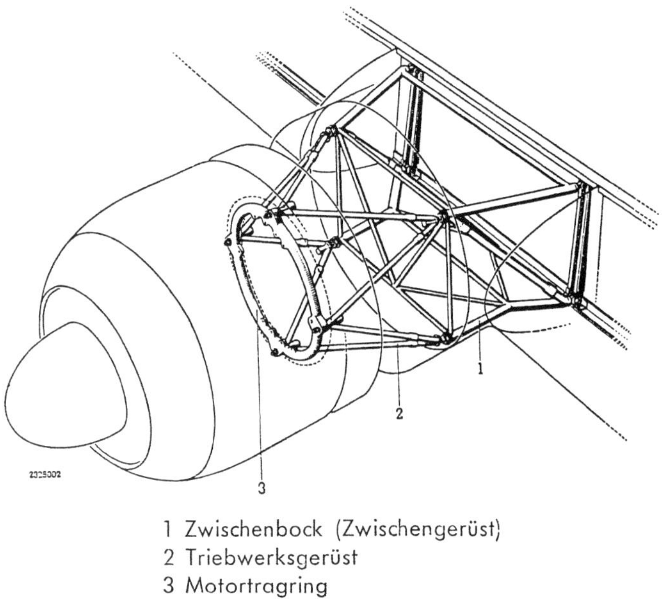

Drawing from *Arado Flugzeugbau* featuring the port *BMW 801A* radial piston engine and its mounting framework to the wing spar.

The starboard *BMW 801A* radial piston engine on the *Arado Ar 232A V1* and featuring its mounting frame work to the wing's main spar.

Close up details of the starboard *BMW 801A* radial engine as mounted to wing of the *Arado Ar 232A V1* prototype.

The starboard side of a *BMW 801D* radial piston engine.

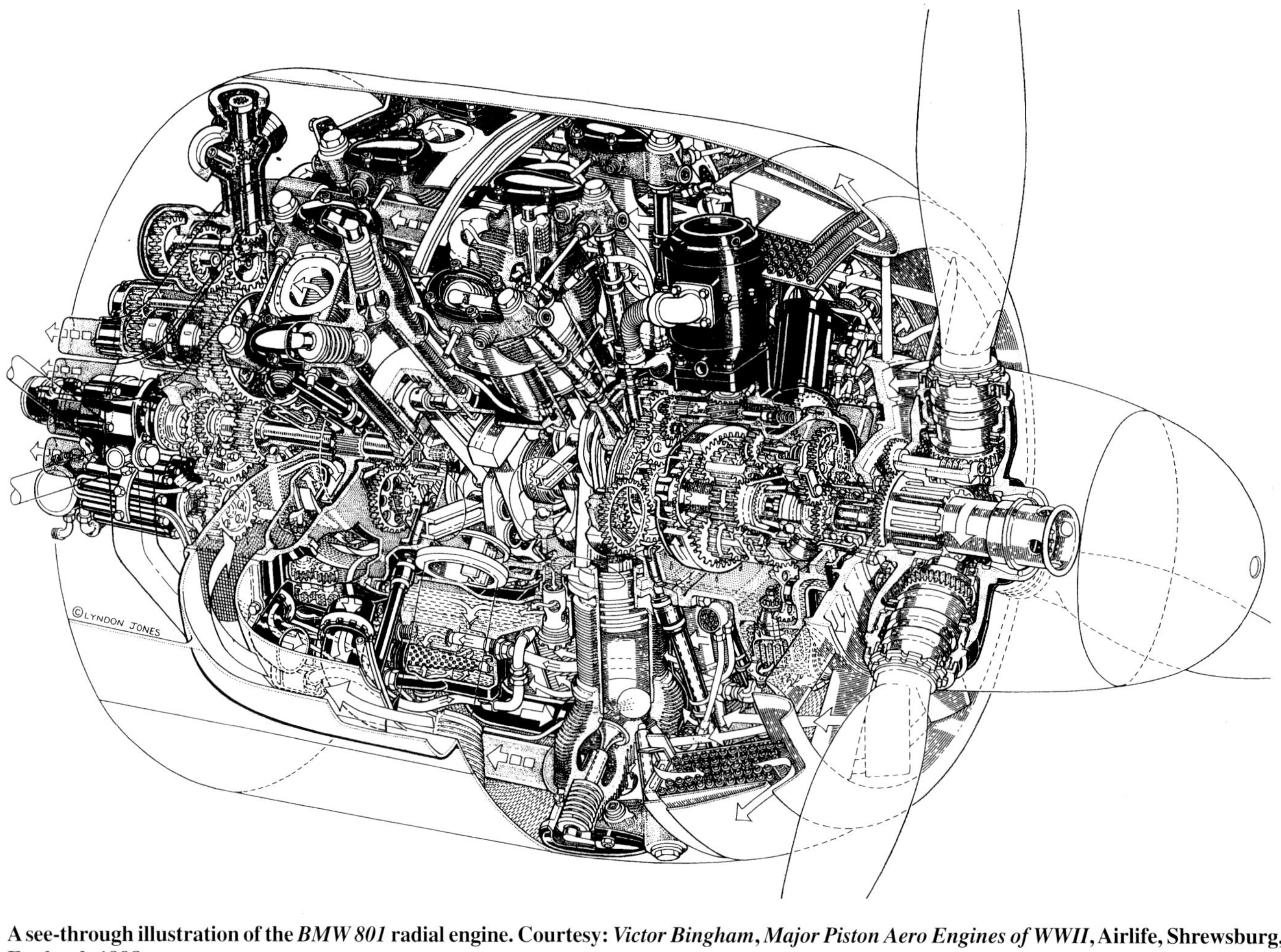

A see-through illustration of the *BMW 801* radial engine. Courtesy: *Victor Bingham, Major Piston Aero Engines of WWII*, Airlife, Shrewsburg, England, 1998.

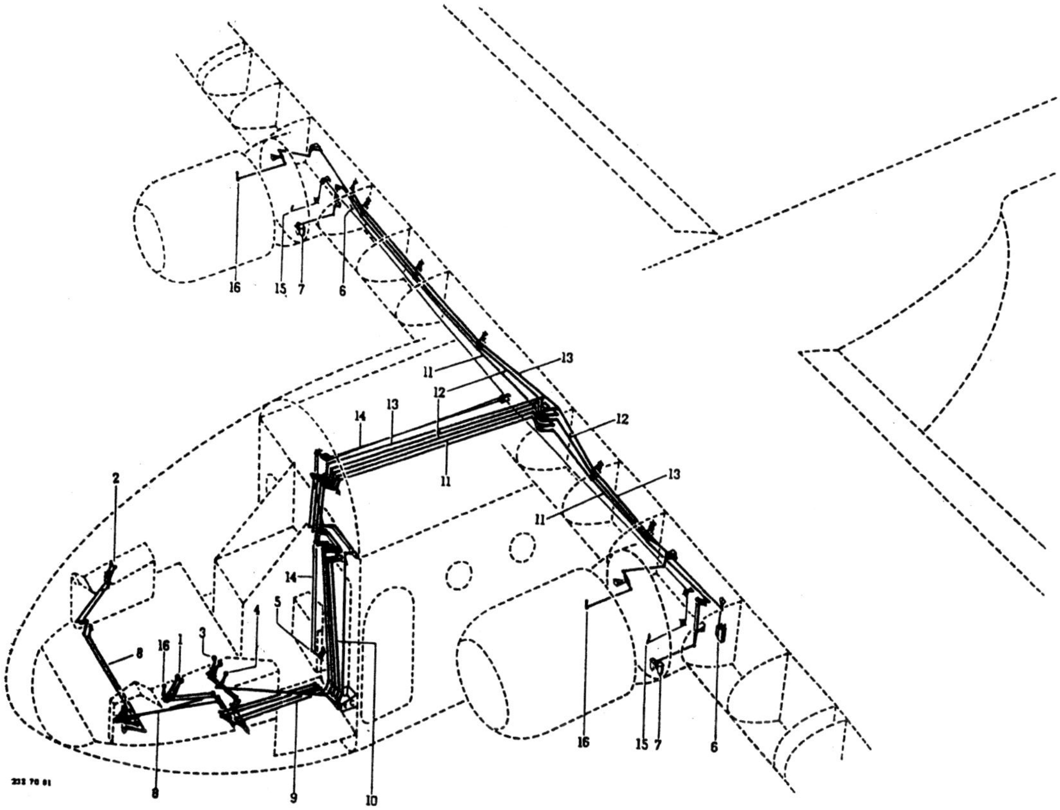

1 Gashebel für Führer
2 Gashebel für Beobachter
3 Brandhahnschalthebel
4 Behälterschalthebel
5 Kaltstartschalthebel
6 Ventilbatterie
7 Filterbrandhahngerät
8 Verbindungsgestänge für das Gasgestänge
9 Bedienungsgestänge unter der linken Bedienbank
10 Bediengestänge am Spant 7
11 Brandhahngestänge
12 Gasgestänge
13 Behälterschaltgestänge
14 Kaltstartzüge
15 Kaltstarthebel (am Motor)
16 Leistungswählhebel (am Motor)

Lageplan des Triebwerksbediengestänges

An illustration from *Arado Flugzeugbau* featuring the control linkage in an *Arado Ar 232A* between the *BMW 801A* radial piston engine and the cockpit.

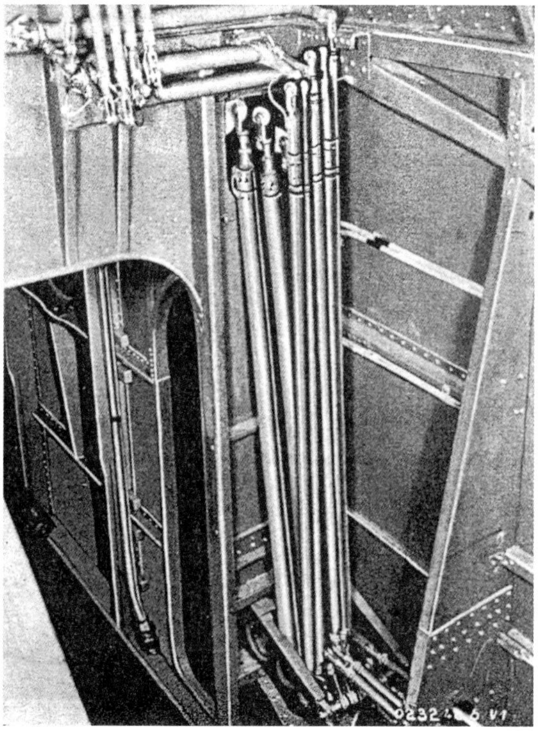

One segment of the engine control linkage in an *Arado Ar 232A* between its *BMW 801A* and the cockpit.

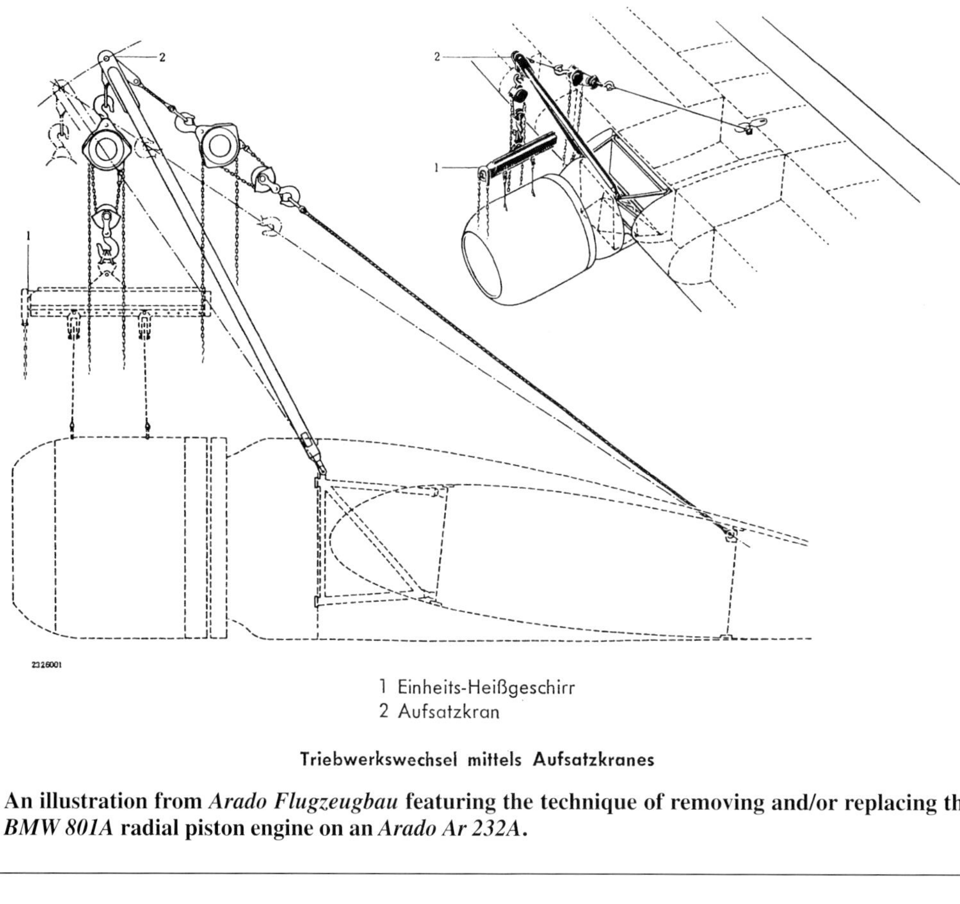

2326001

1 Einheits-Heißgeschirr
2 Aufsatzkran

Triebwerkswechsel mittels Aufsatzkranes

An illustration from *Arado Flugzeugbau* featuring the technique of removing and/or replacing the *BMW 801A* radial piston engine on an *Arado Ar 232A*.

A starboard side view of an *Arado Ar 232A* with its full span wing "*Arado* traveling flaps." *Arado* had been developing these landing aids since 1938, and they had been fitted to an *Arado Ar 240 Zerstörer*. The traveling flaps increased the wing area by 25 percent. Scale model and photographed by *Günter Sengfelder.*

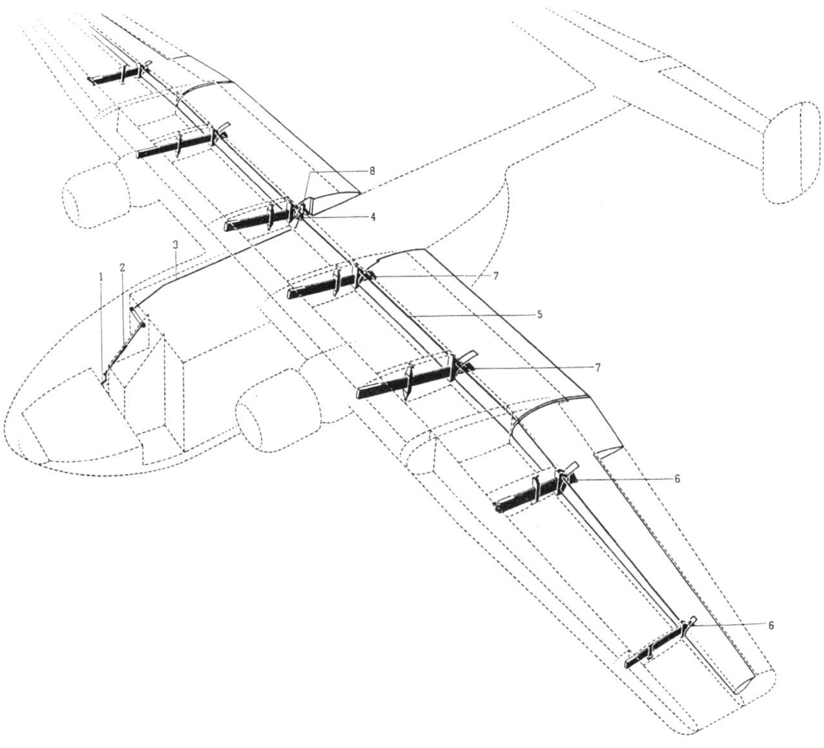

An illustration from *Arado Flugzeugbau* featuring the internal wing support structure for its "traveling wing flaps" on the *Arado Ar 232A* combat zone transport.

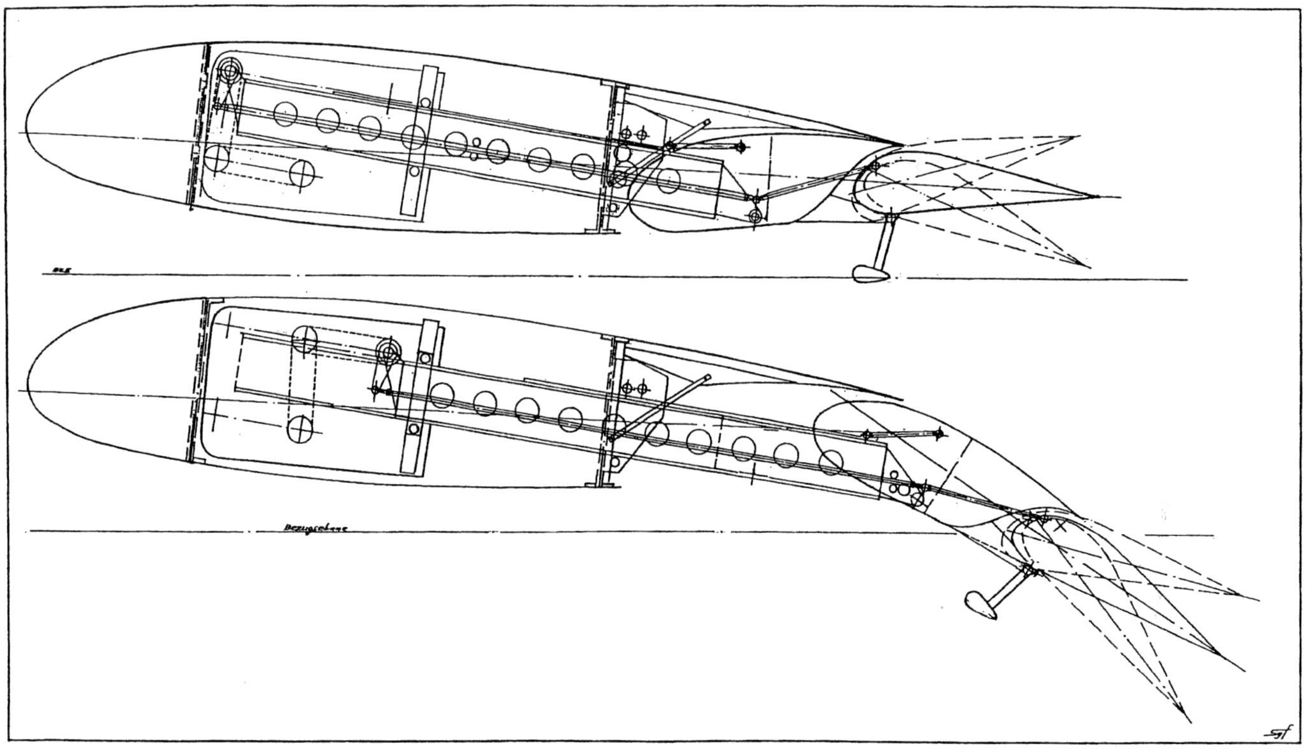

An illustration from *Arado Flugzeugbau* featuring the internal wing support structure for the "traveling wing flaps" on their *Arado Ar 232A*.

An *Arado Ar 232B*, the four engined combat zone transport, featuring its starboard side rear and its inboard "*Arado* traveling wing flaps." It is not quite clear what the reason was for all these well-dressed men gathered around this *Ar 232B*, or the reason for the thirteen men up on its wing and dorsal fuselage. Perhaps it was the design and engineering group involved in the *Arado Ar 232* program.

An *Arado Ar 232A* with radio call code *TC+EF* with its "*Arado* traveling wing flaps" shown fully extended. Scale model and photographed by *Günter Sengfelder.*

The starboard side wing of an *Arado Ar 232A* with its "*Arado* traveling wing flap" fully extended.

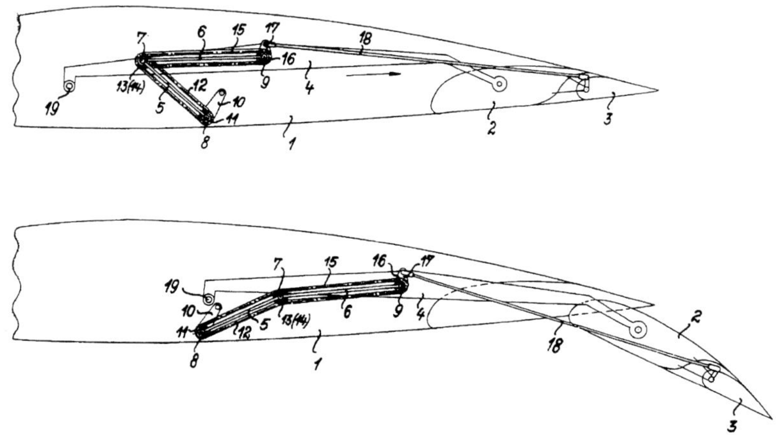

An illustration featuring the "*Arado* traveling wing flap." The upper illustration shows the traveling wing flap fully retracted. The bottom illustration shows the traveling wing flap fully extended.

Arado's* traveling wing flap as seen from the ground. Seen on the starboard wing of an *Arado Ar 234A V1.

Arado's* traveling wing flap seen further extended from the ground. Seen on the starboard wing of the *Arado Ar 232A V1.

Arado's* traveling wing flap seen from the ground is further extended. Seen on the port wing of the *Arado Ar 232A V1.

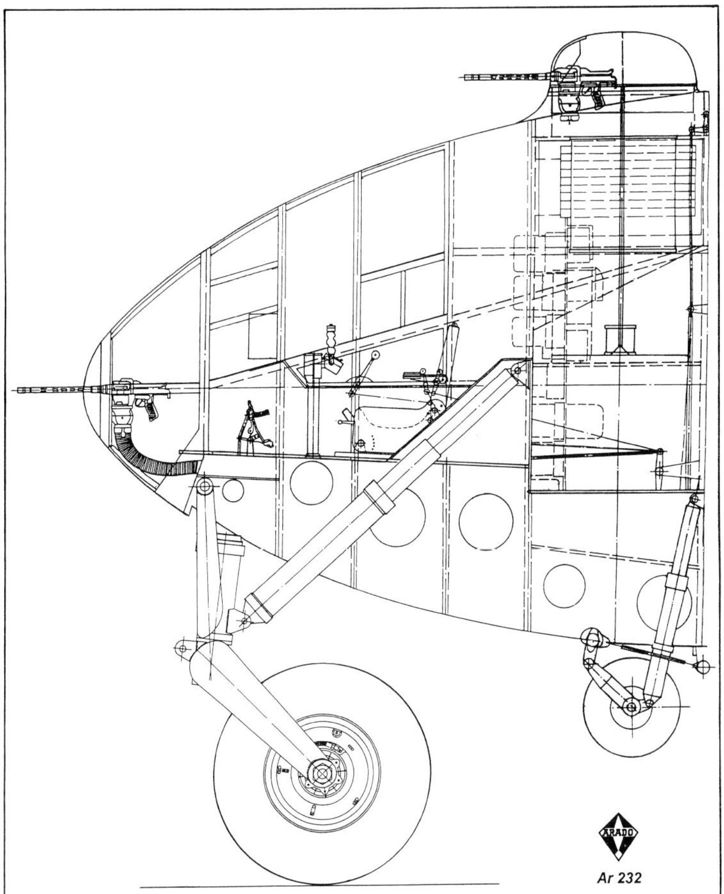

An illustration redrawn from an *Arado Flugzeugbau* copy of the port side nose section of an *Arado Ar 232A* and featuring its nose wheel gear and tire in full extension. Drawing by *Günter Sengfelder.*

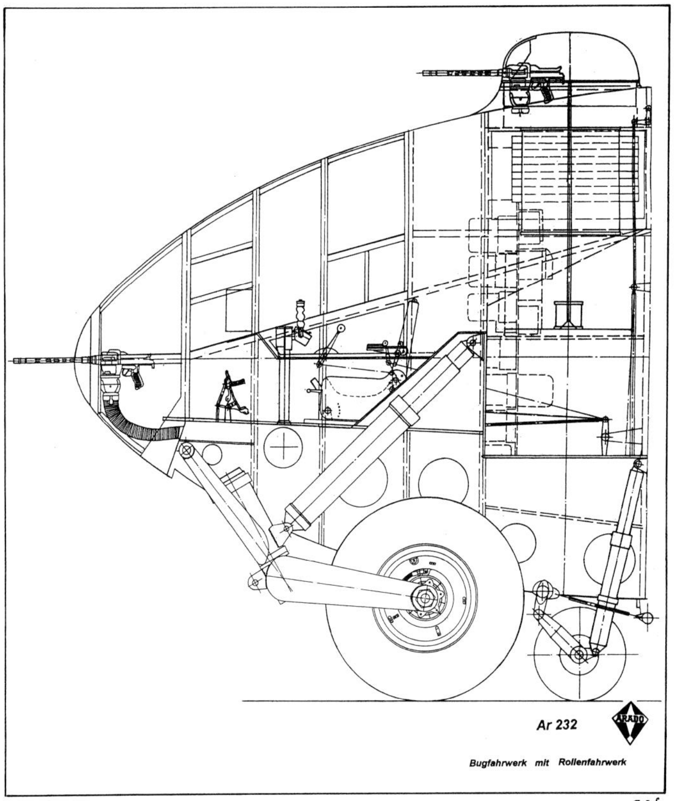

232-2 c Sgf

An illustration redrawn from an *Arado Flugzeugbau* copy of the port side nose section of their *Arado Ar 232A* and featuring its nose wheel gear and tire in partial retraction in order to lower the flying machine down to its 11 rows of caterpillar-like fuselage-mounted tires. Drawing by *Günter Sengfelder.*

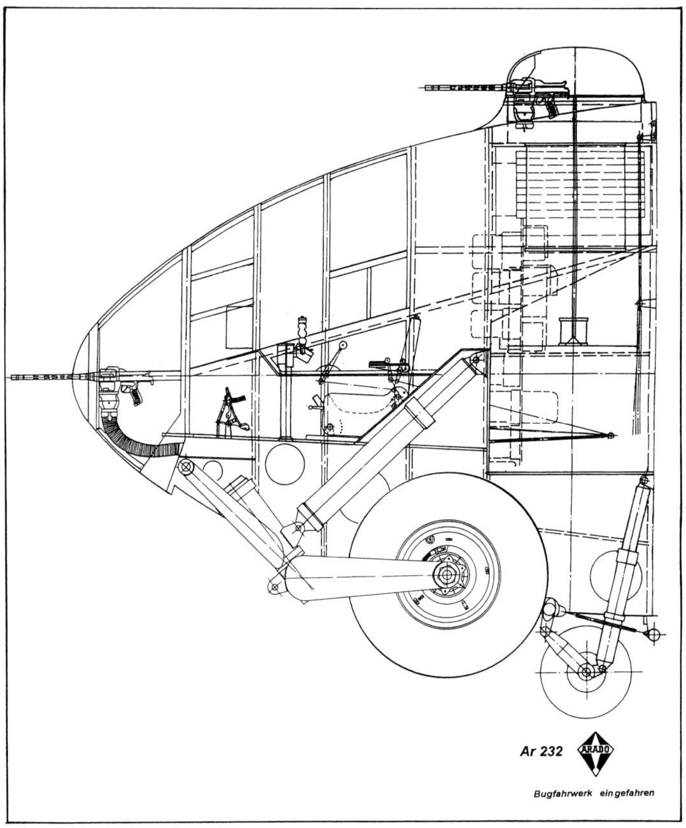

c Sgf

An illustration redrawn from an *Arado Flugzeugbau* copy of the port side nose section of their *Arado Ar 232A* and featuring its nose wheel gear and tire in full retraction. Drawing by *Günter Sengfelder.*

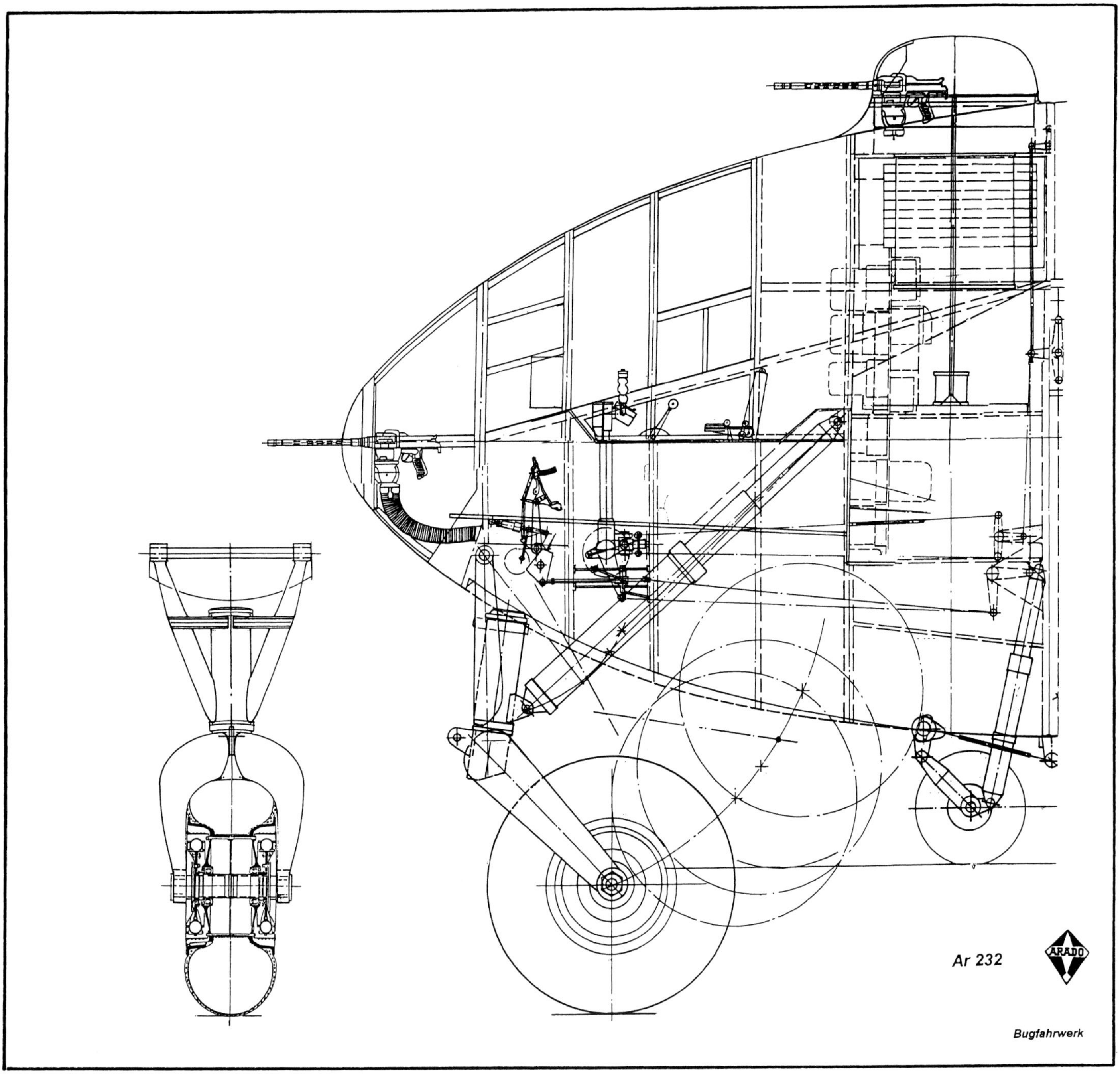

An illustration from *Arado Flugzeugbau* featuring the full range of the nose wheel gear and tire from full extension to full retraction. To the left of the illustration is a rear view of the nose wheel support fork and gear attachment.

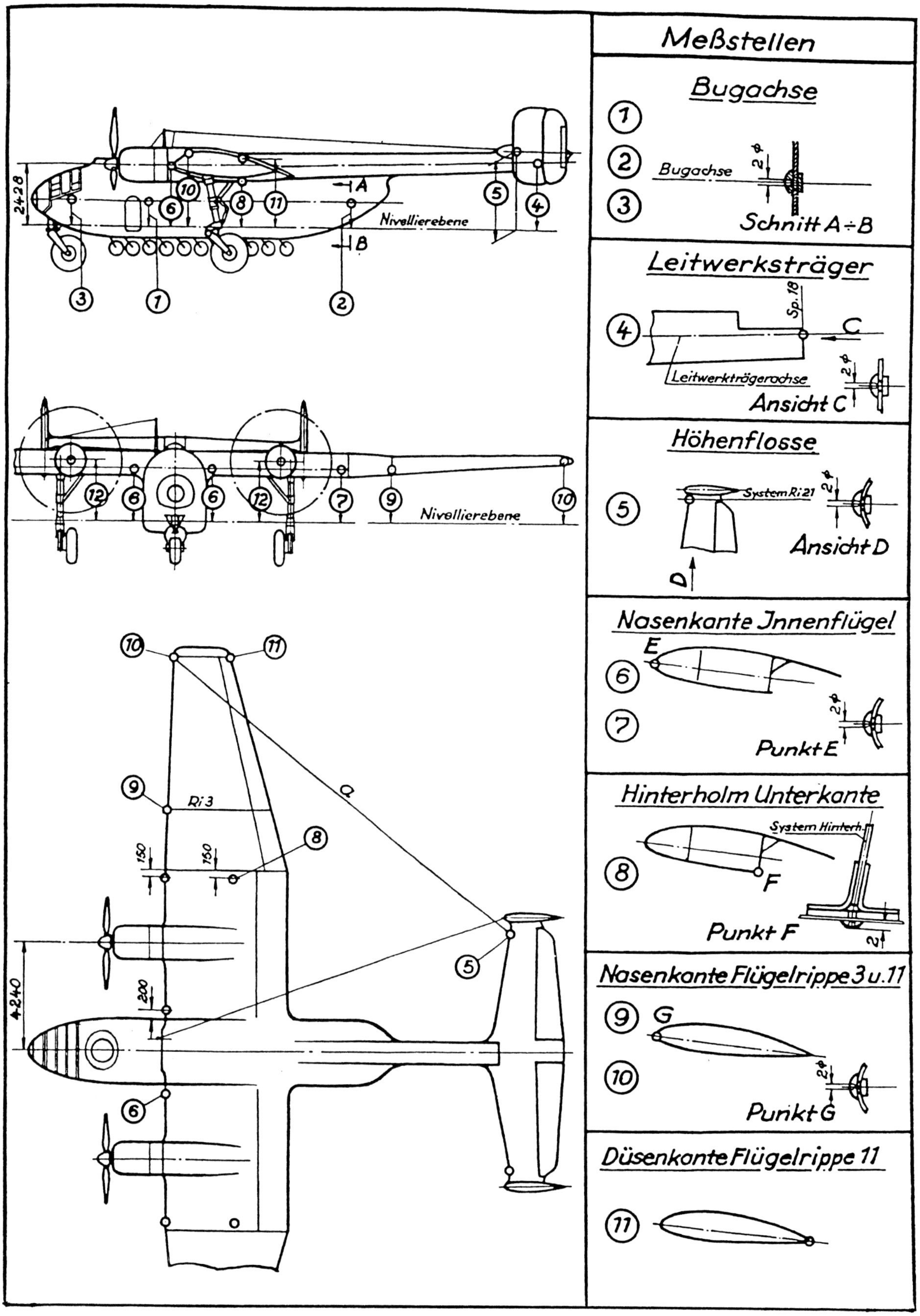

A 3-view illustration of the *Arado Ar 232A* with various points of reference.

The *Arado Ar 232A V1's* cargo bay under construction as seen from its starboard side with the cockpit to the far right.

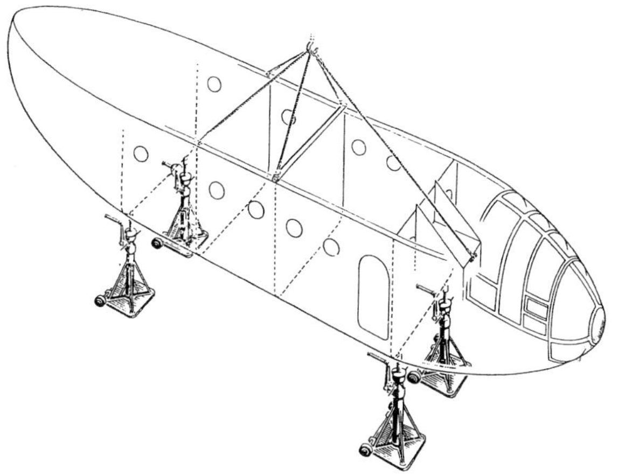

A see-through illustration from *Arado Flugzeugbau* of the cargo bay on the *Arado* Ar *232A V1* and *V2.*

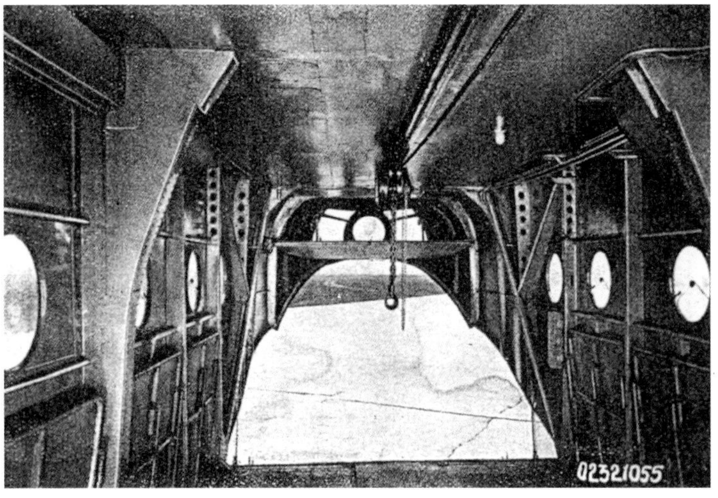

The interior cargo bay of the *Arado Ar 232A V1* looking aft from the cockpit. The white area in the photo is the hydraulically operated cargo door. At the top of the cargo bay the interior crane can be seen.

The interior cargo bay of the *Arado Ar 232A V1* looking aft from the cockpit. The cargo bay has been arranged to transport troops, which would sit on the fold down metal seats.

The *Arado Ar 232A* carried a ladder mounted in the cargo bay for entering and leaving the cargo bay port side hatch.

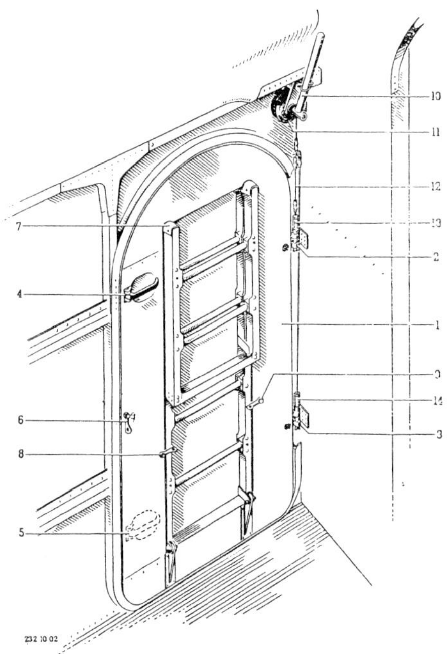

An illustration from *Arado Flugzeugbau* featuring the port side cargo bay hatch. Notice that in this illustration, the ladder is attached directly to the inside door/ hatch.

A port side view of the *Arado Ar 232A V1*, its cargo bay hatch and the ladder in place.

An illustration from *Arado Flugzeugbau* featuring the dimensions of the cargo bay on the *Arado Ar 232A* and *Ar 232B*.

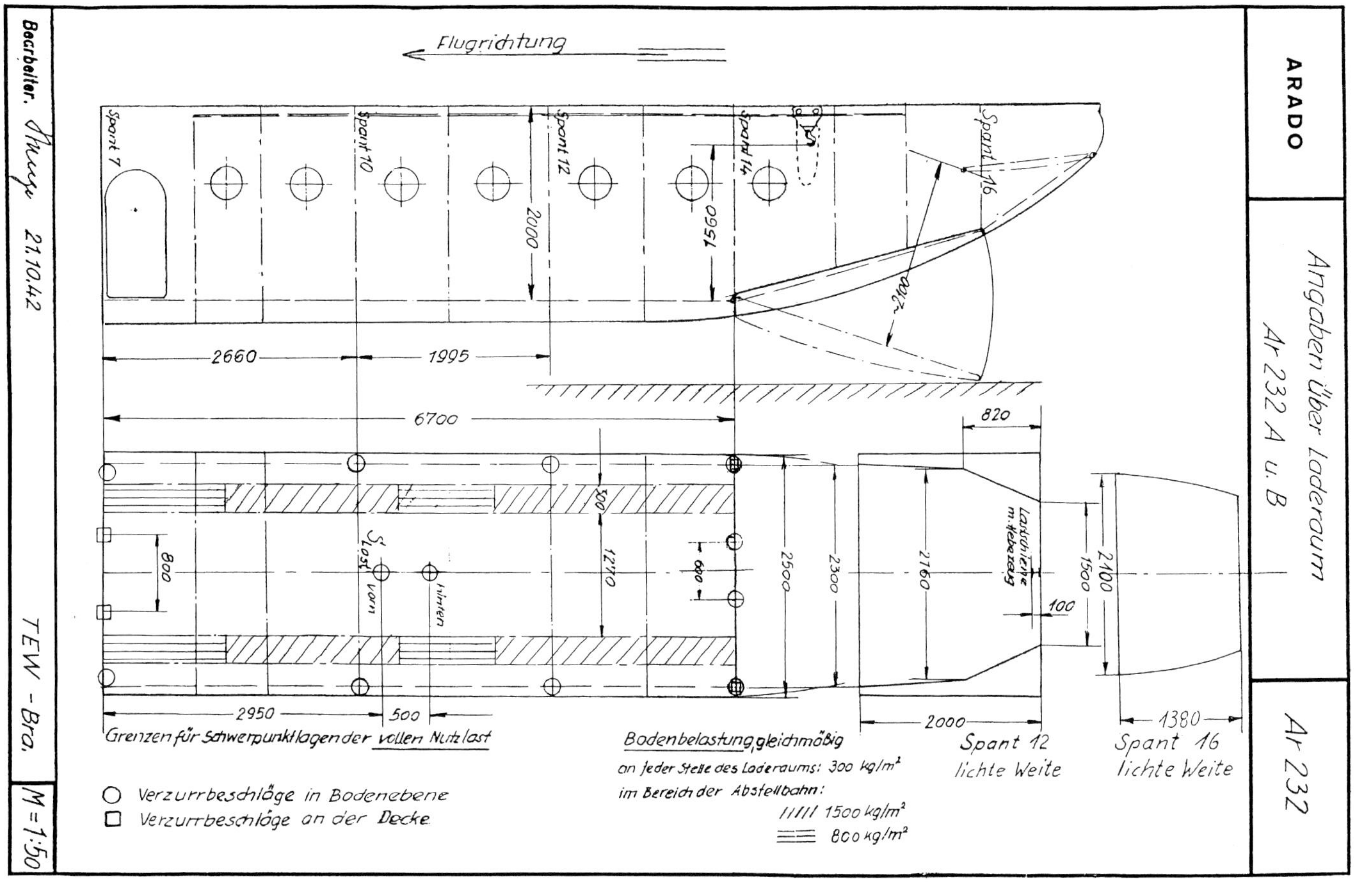

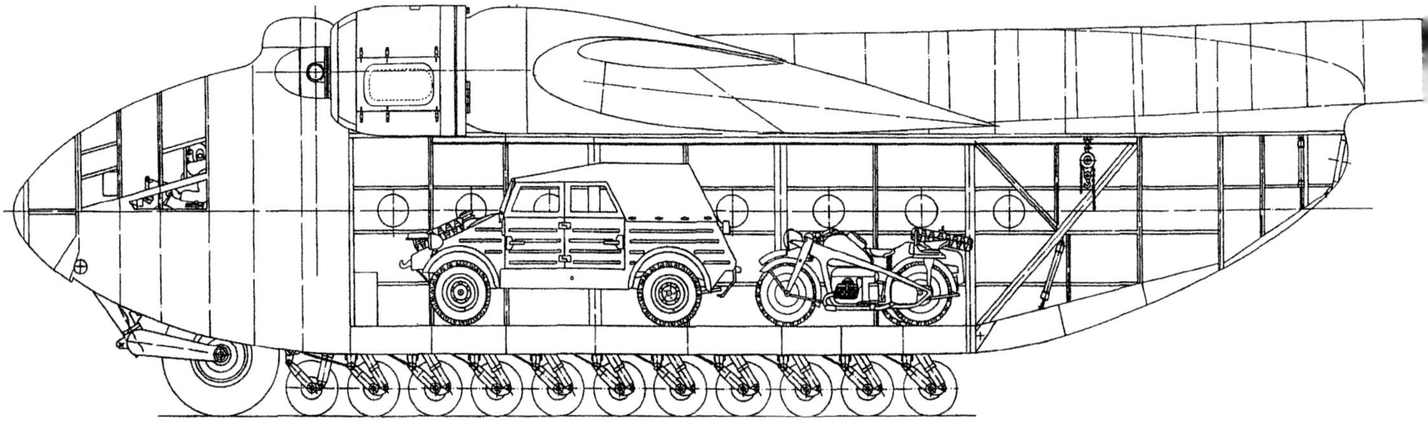

A see-through illustration of the port side cargo bay of an *Arado Ar 232A* showing how a *Kubelwagon* staff auto and motorcycle would be accommodated. Drawing by *Günter Sengfelder.*

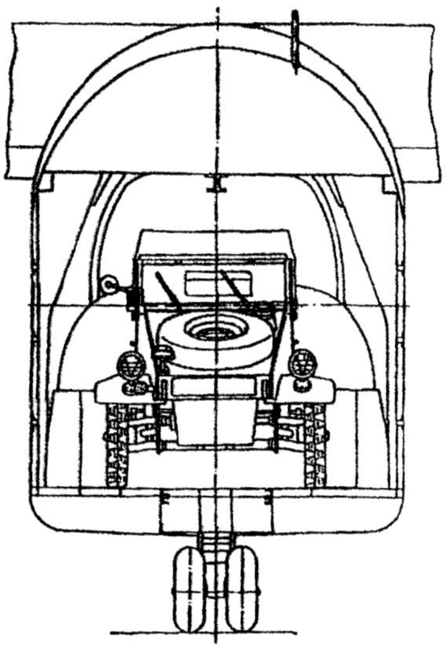

An illustration showing how the *Kubelwagon* would fit inside the *Ar 232A's* cargo bay. Drawing by *Günter Sengfelder.*

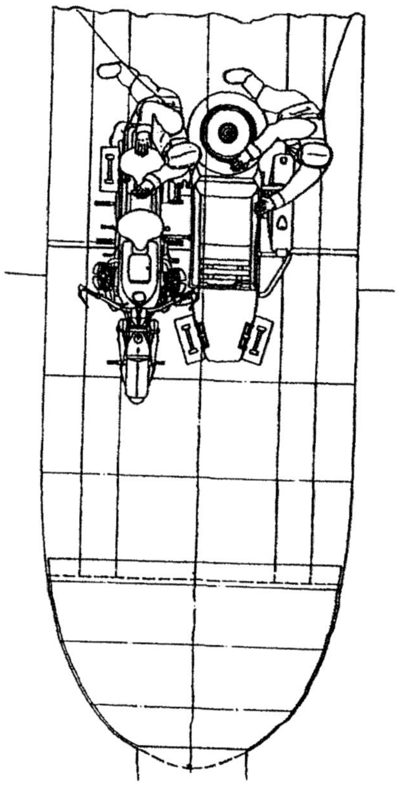

An illustration showing how the motorcycle would fit inside the *Ar 232A's* cargo bay. Drawing by *Günter Sengfelder.*

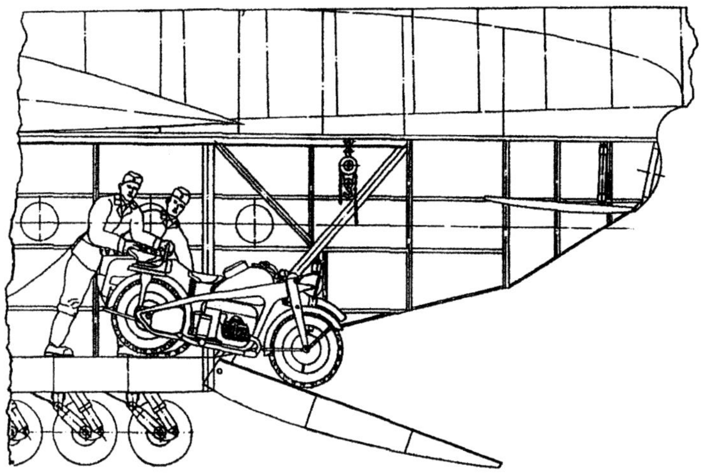

Off-loading the cargo in the *Arado Ar 232A* shown above was easy due to the cargo bay ramp. Drawing by *Günter Sengfelder.*

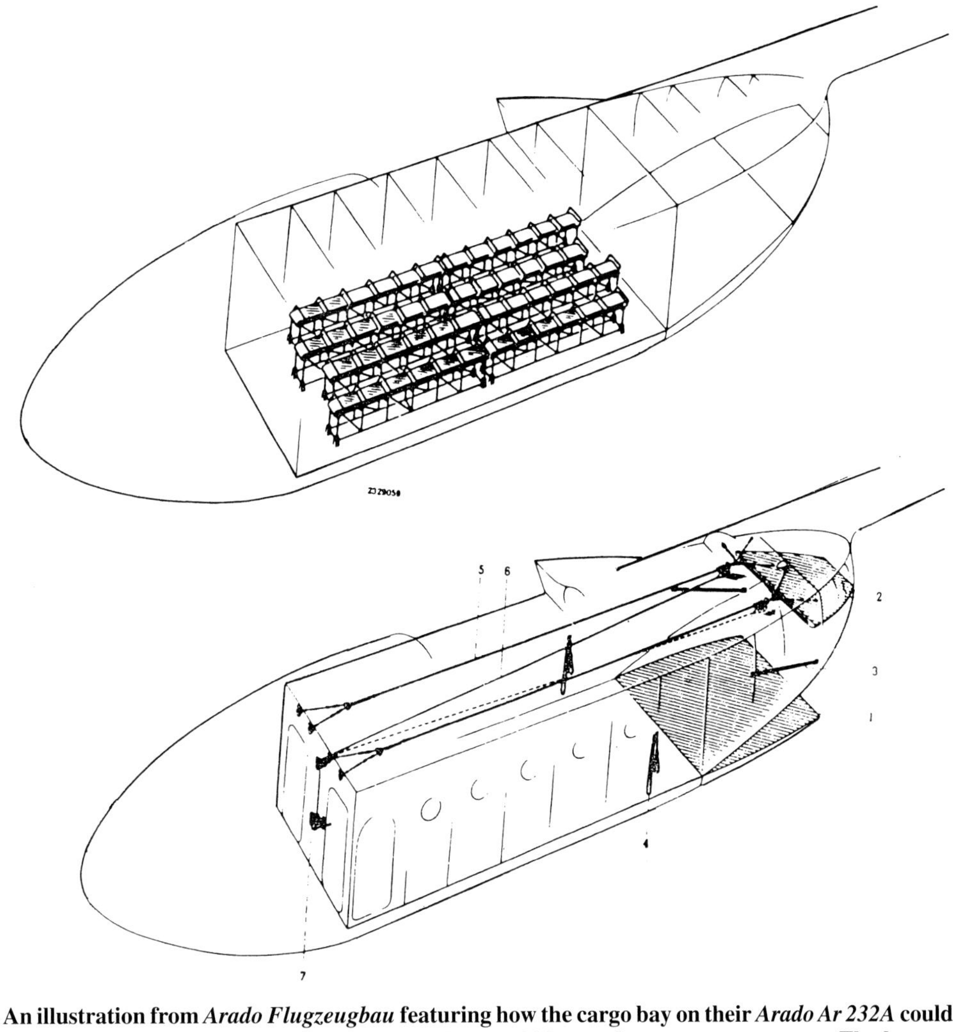

An illustration from *Arado Flugzeugbau* featuring how the cargo bay on their *Arado Ar 232A* could be utilized. Top image shows how the cargo bay could be used as a troop transport. The bottom image features a cargo container-like item that is moved in and out via a system of cables and pulleys.

The *Arado Ar 232A* with its cargo bay door in the full up position. Scale model and photographed by *Günter Sengfelder.*

Arado Flugzeugbau did a nice job designing the cargo bay door on their *Ar 232A*, as seen in this starboard side rear view. Scale model and photographed by *Günter Sengfelder.*

Arado Flugzeugbau design engineers chose a simple box-like container, as shown in this pen and ink starboard side illustration, for their *Arado Ar 232A* cargo bay. The cargo bay door is shown open.

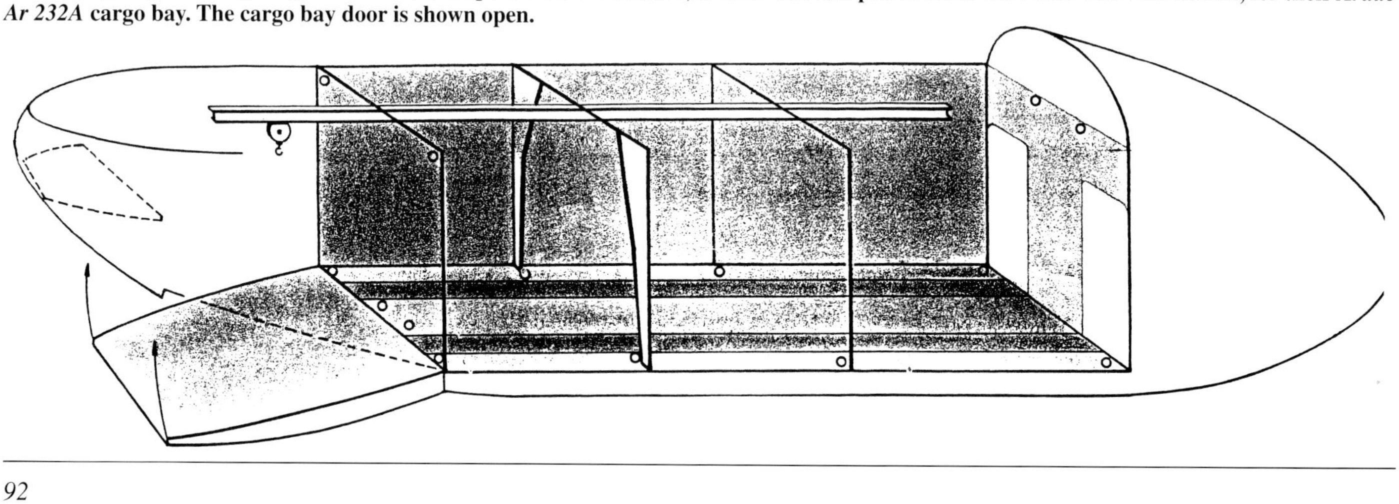

A port side rear view of an *Arado Ar 232A* undergoing off-loading operations via its open rear cargo bay door. Scale model and photographed by *Günter Sengfelder.*

A port side rear view of an *Arado Ar 232A* undergoing loading operations via its open rear cargo bay door. A *Junkers Jumo 004B* turbojet engine appears next to be loaded, while a *Volkswagen* staff auto awaits its turn to be driven up the ramp and into the cargo bay. Scale model and photographed by *Günter Sengfelder.*

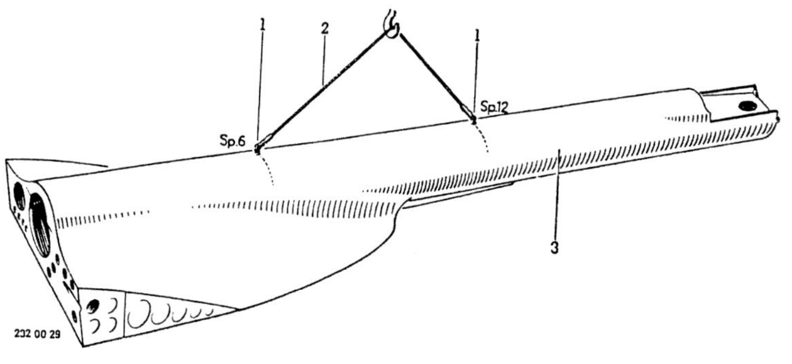

An illustration from *Arado Flugzeugbau* featuring the lifting eyes on the *Arado Ar 232A's* tail boom.

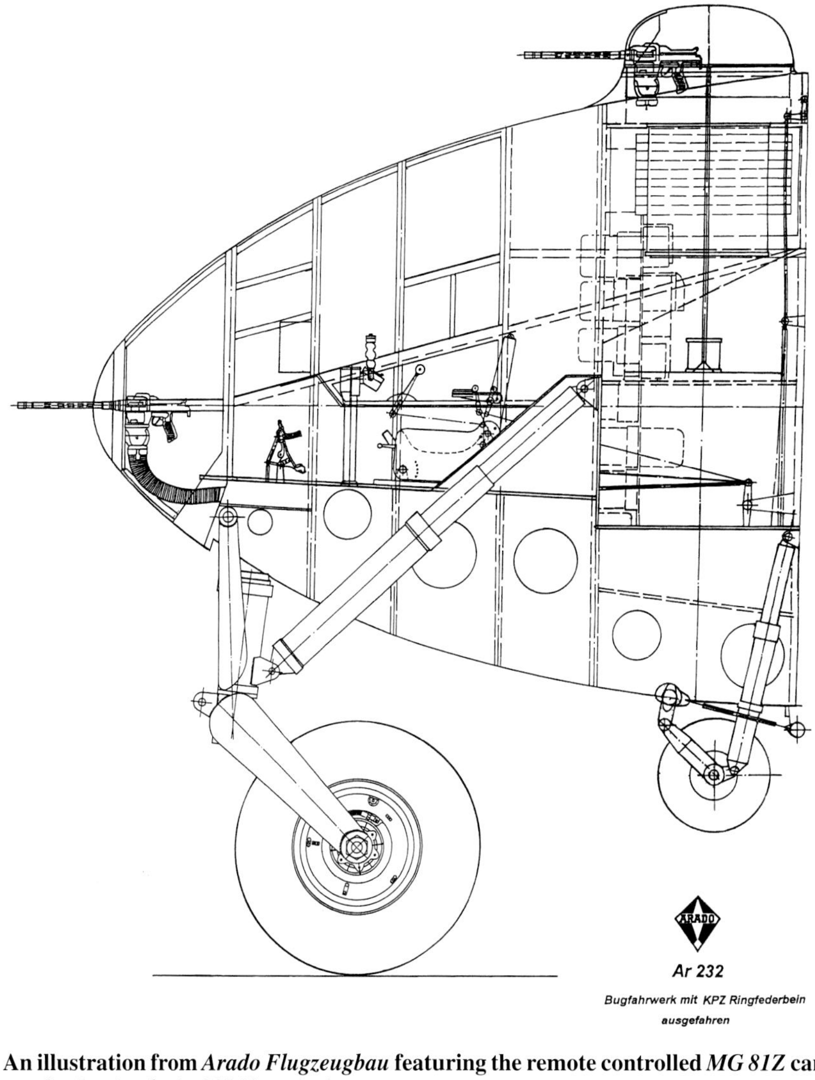

An illustration from *Arado Flugzeugbau* featuring the remote controlled *MG 81Z* cannon in the *Arado Ar 232A's* cockpit nose.

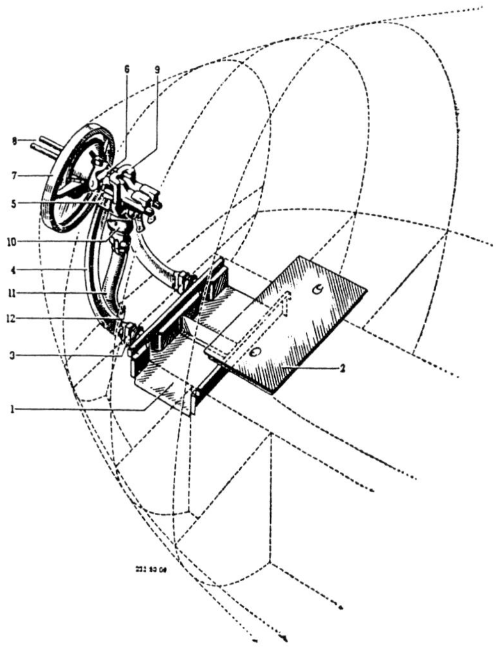

1 Gurtkasten
2 Gurtkastendeckel
3 Zuführungsstück
4 Gurtzuführungsschlauch
5 Gurtzuführung
6 Lagerkugel (ohne VE 38)
7 Waffenlagerung
8 MG 81 Z
9 Hülsenabführungsstück
10 Hülsenkasten
11 Hülsenschlauch
12 Schelle für Schlauchhalterung

Abb. 1: **Waffenanlage A-Stand**

An illustration from *Arado Flugzeugbau* featuring the remote controlled *MG 81Z* cannon in the *Arado Ar 232A's* cockpit nose. The metal box aft the *MG 81Z* would contain the belted shells.

The remote controlled *MG 81Z* cannon mounted in the nose section of the *Arado Ar 232A's* cockpit.

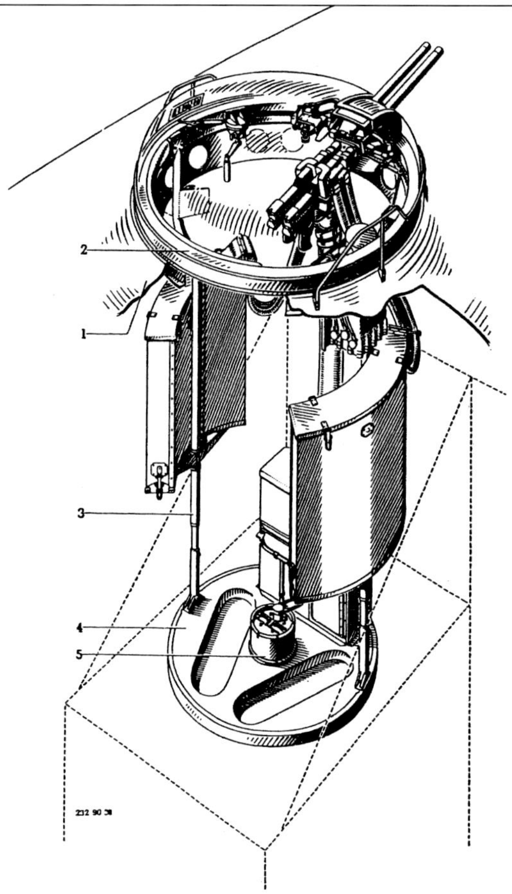

1 Ringspant-Aufbau im Rumpfoberteil
2 Drehkranzlafette
3 Schützenstand
4 Fußplatte
5 Lagerung

Abb. 2: **Waffenanlage B-Stand**

An illustration from *Arado Flugzeugbau* featuring the dorsal fuselage mounted manned 7.92 mm *MG 81* machine gun turret in the *Arado Ar 232A*.

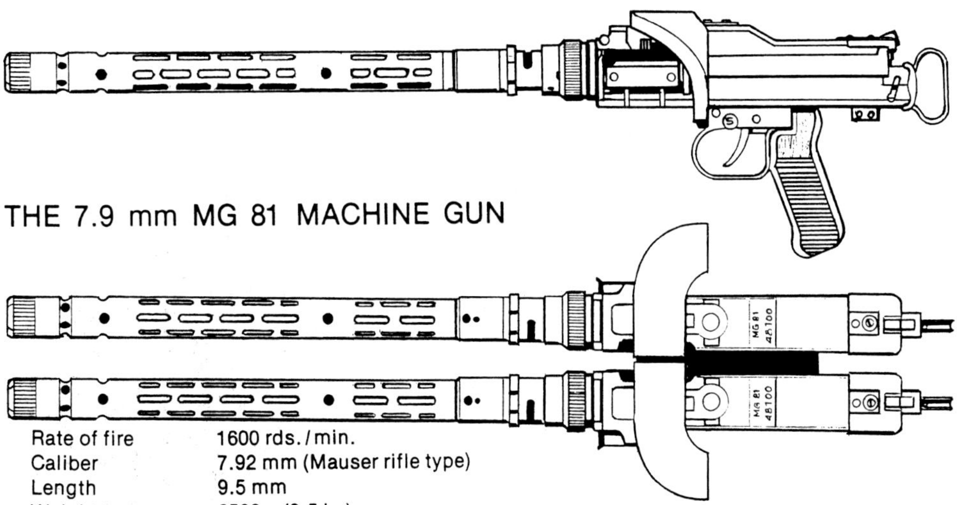

Rate of fire	1600 rds./min.
Caliber	7.92 mm (Mauser rifle type)
Length	9.5 mm
Weight	6500 g (6.5 kg)
Ammo feed	belt
Muzzle velocity	705 m/second
Mauser	1938

An illustration of the manned 7.92 mm *MG 81* machine gun of the type installed on the dorsal fuselage of an *Arado Ar 232A*.

The *MG 81* machine gun (7.92 mm *Mauser* rifle type) with gunner of the type featured on the *Arado Ar 232A* dorsal turret.

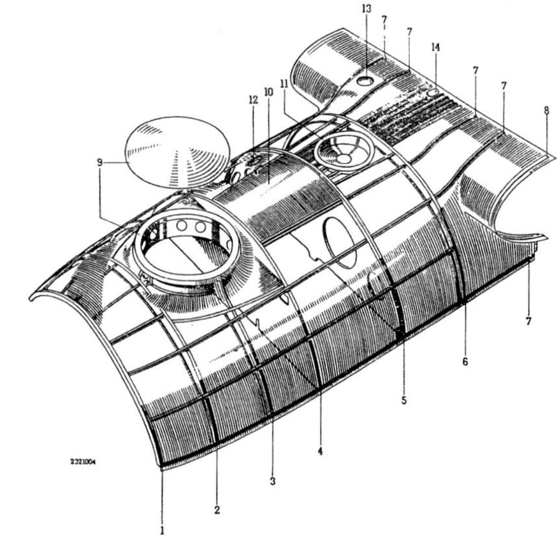

1–2 Spantbogen
3 Geteilte Spantbogen
4–5 Vollspanten
6 Spantbogen
7 Längsstringer
8 Übergangsstück zum Flügelmittelteil an der Beplankung
9 Ringspant-Aufbau für Drehkranzlafette mit Abschlußdeckel
10 Notausstiegklappe
11 Wanne für Peilrahmen
12 Durchgang für Antennenmast
13 Durchgang für Antennenzuführung
14 Handlochdeckel

Rumpfoberteil

An illustration from *Arado Flugzeugbau* featuring the dorsal fuselage mounting for the crew operated *MG 81Z* cannon turret on an *Arado Ar 232A*. The *MG 81Z* cannon turret is located just aft of the cockpit.

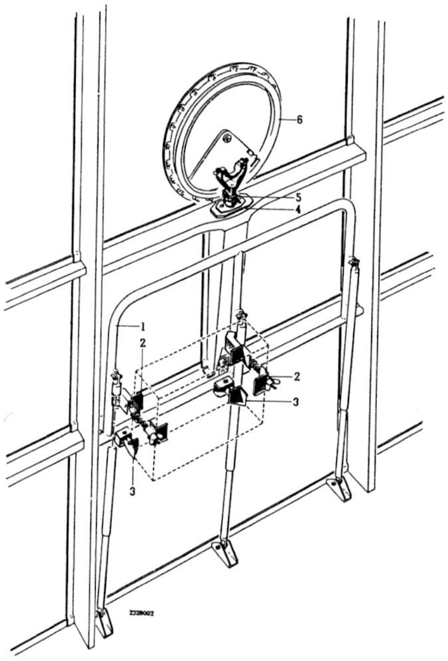

1 Klappsitz
2 Festspannvorrichtung für den Vollgurtkasten
3 Böckchen zum Aufsetzen des Vollgurtkastens
4 Lafettenlagerung
5 Pivotzapfen
6 Fenster mit drehbarer Scheibe

Abb. 4: **Einbau der Fensterlafette**

An illustration from *Arado Flugzeugbau* featuring the cannon mounting hardware for mounting a single 7.9 mm *MG 34* infantry machine gun in the window of an *Arado Ar 232A*. As many as eight of the windows would accept an *MG 34* machine gun

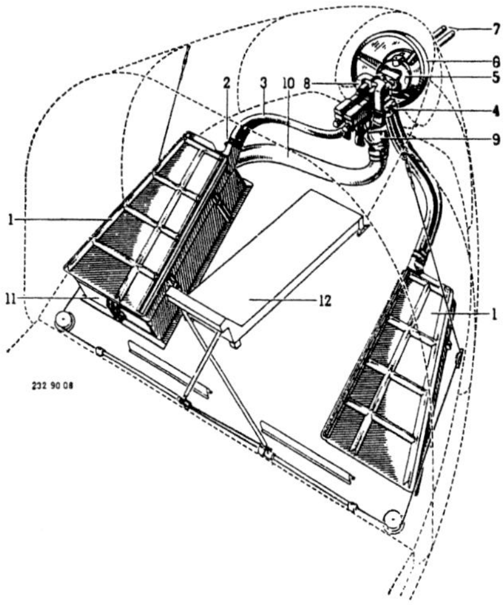

1 Patronenkasten
2 Zuführungsstück
3 Gurtzuführungsschlauch
4 Gurtzuführung
5 Lagerkugel (ohne VE 33)
6 Waffenlagerung
7 MG 81 Z
8 Hülsenabführungsstück
9 Hülsenkasten
10 Hülsenabführungsschlauch
11 Leerhülsen- und Gurtkasten
12 Pritsche mit Verstellagerung

Abb. 3: **Waffenlager C-Stand**

An illustration from *Arado Flugzeugbau* featuring the components of the remote controlled *MG 81Z* cannon located in the rear fuselage above the loading ramp.

The rear fuselage mounted *MG 81Z* remote controlled cannon seen directly beneath the forward portion of the tail boom. Scale model and photographed by *Günter Sengfelder.*

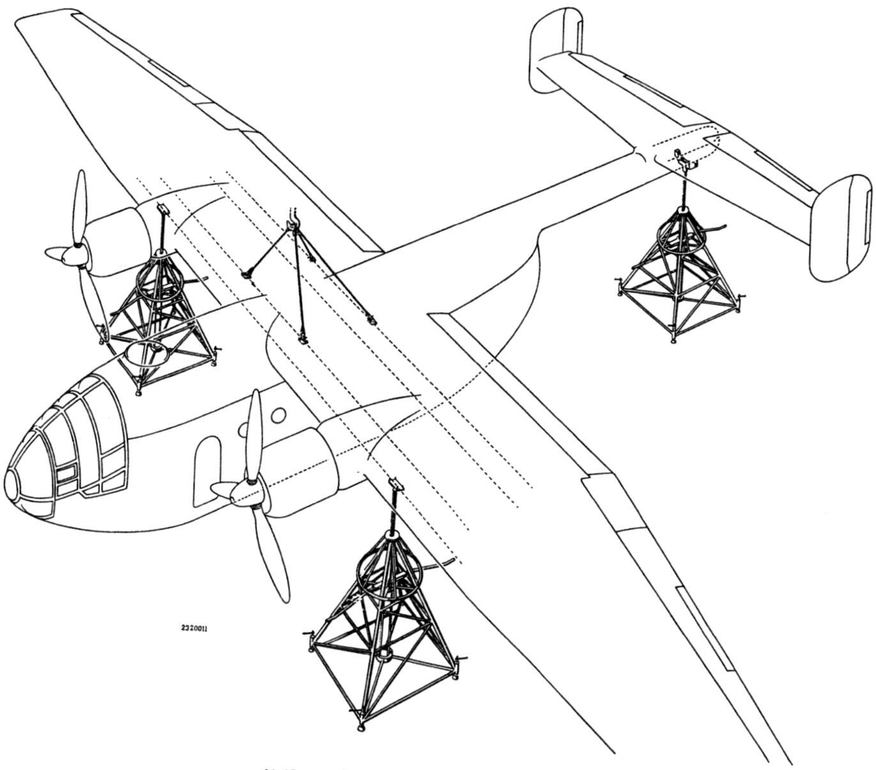

Heißen und Aufbocken des ganzen Flugzeuges

An illustration from *Arado Flugzeugbau* featuring lifting attachment points needed to lift the entire aircraft in order to place it on three steel pipe support stands.

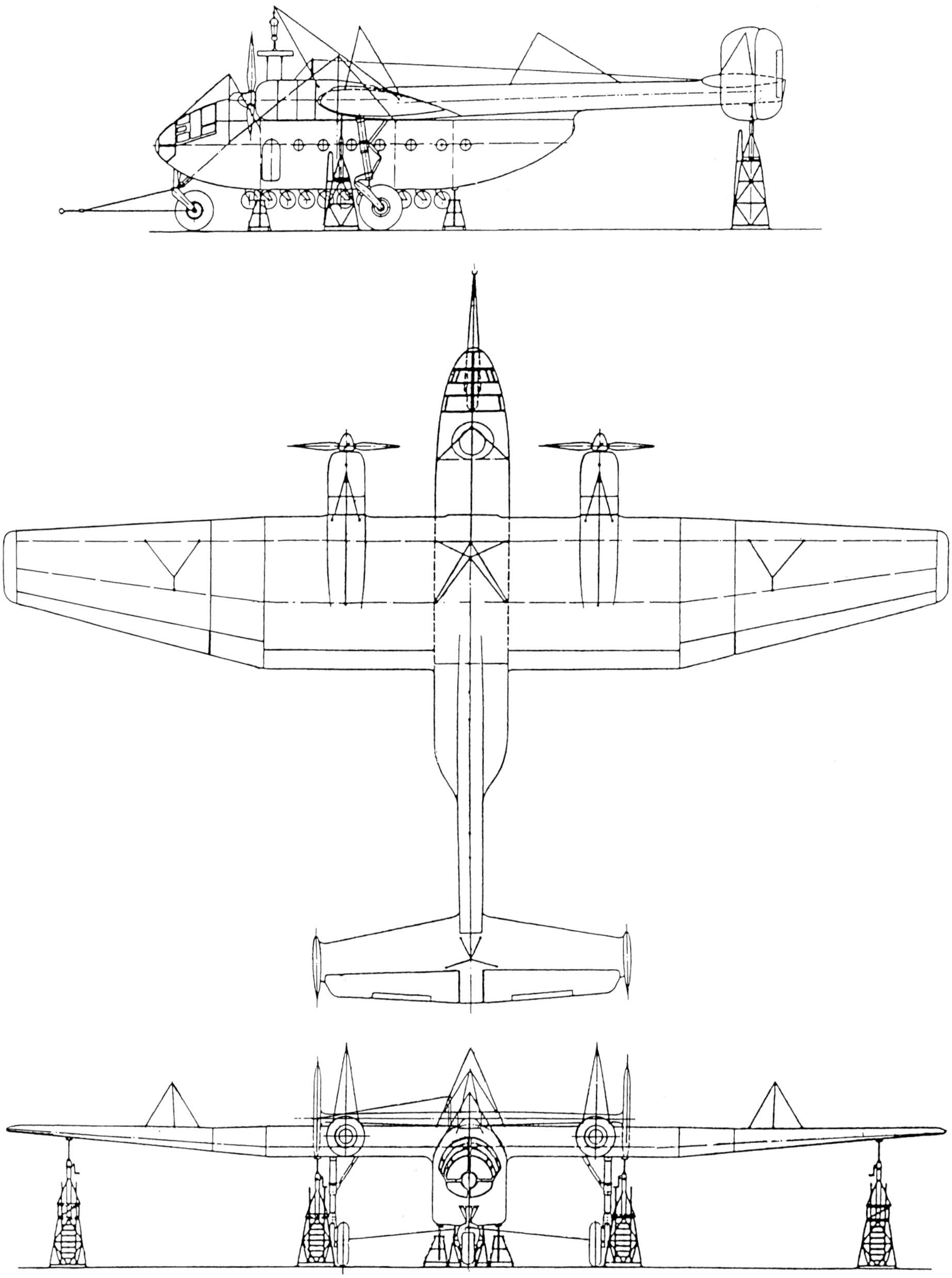

An illustration from *Arado Flugzeugbau* featuring the various lifting points on the *Arado Ar 232A*, such as engines, outer wing panels, and the entire aircraft itself.

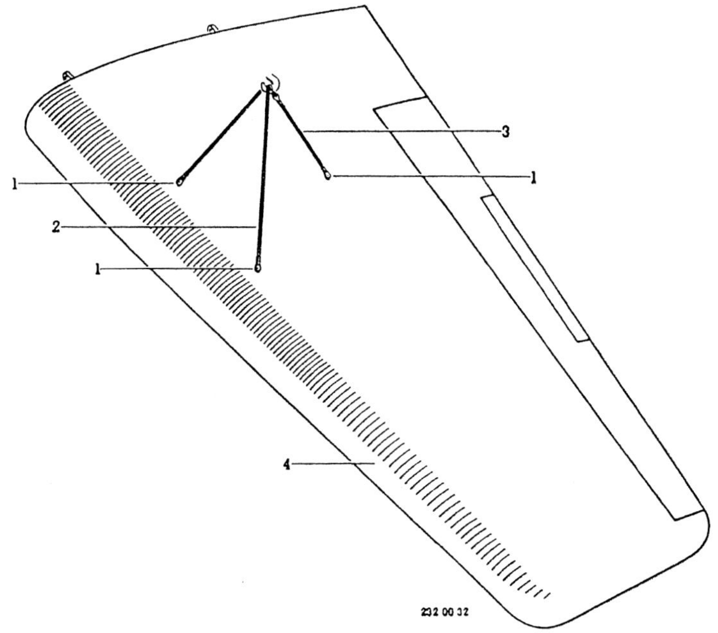

1 Ringschraube
2 Vorderes Seil mit Klemmösen
3 Hinteres Seil mit Klemm- und Aufhängeöse
4 Außenflügel

Heißvorrichtung am Außenflügel

This illustration from *Arado Flugzeugbau* illustrates how the outer wing panel from an *Arado Ar 232A* should be lifted via lifting eyes in the upper surface of the wing panel.

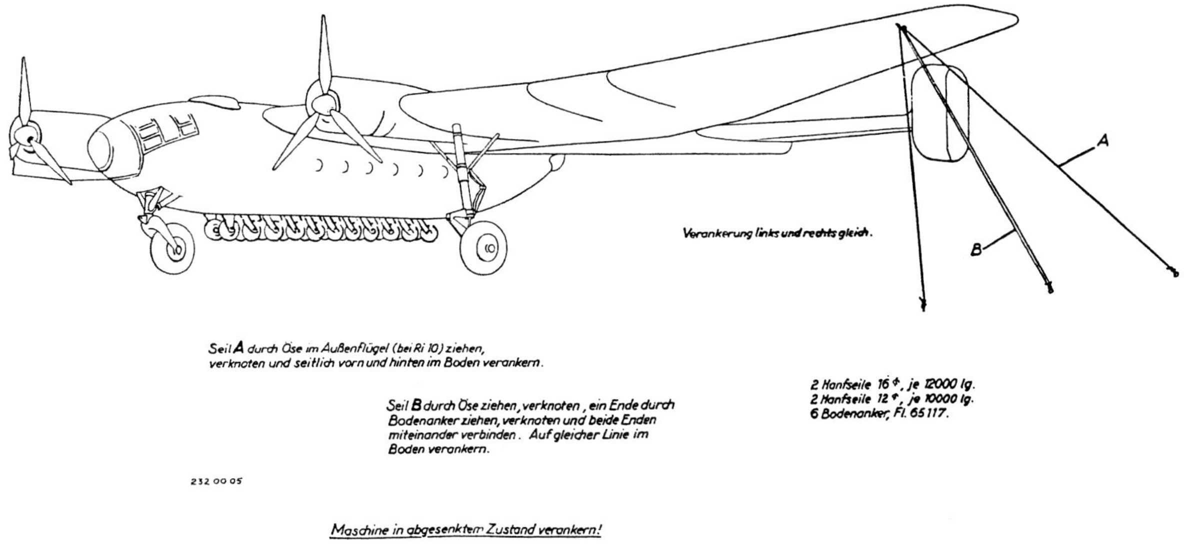

Flugzeug nur mit eingefahrenen Landeflügeln verankern

Verankerungsplan

This illustration from *Arado Flugzeugbau* illustrates how an *Arado Ar 232A* should be tied down using a rope attachment fitted into the wing near the wing tip.

An *Arado Ar 232A* shown after landing with its "*Arado* wing area-increasing flaps" still in their full down position. Scale model and photographed by *Günter Sengfelder.*

An overhead view of the above image. Scale model and photographed by *Günter Sengfelder.*

An *Arado Ar 232A* with its "*Arado* wing area-increasing flap" seen here in its full down position. Scale model and photographed by *Günter Sengfelder.*

An *Arado Ar 232A* in the process of retracting its "*Arado* wing area-increasing flap." Scale model and photographed by *Günter Sengfelder.*

A nose-on view of an *Arado Ar 232A* with its "*Arado* wing area-increasing flaps" in their full retracted position. Scale model and photographed by *Günter Sengfelder.*

A view of the above image with its "*Arado* wing area-increasing flaps" in their full extended position. Scale model and photographed by *Günter Sengfelder.*

A port-side nose view of an *Arado Ar 232A* with its "*Arado* wing area-increasing flaps" in the full down position. Scale model and photographed by *Günter Sengfelder.*

The same *Arado Ar 232A* with its "*Arado* wing area-increasing flaps" in the full retracted position. Scale model and photographed by *Günter Sengfelder.*

The quantity of goods and supplies which could be packed inside the *Arado Ar 232A's* cargo bay was substantial. Scale model and photographed by *Günter Sengfelder.*

Included in the cargo to be loaded on board this *Arado Ar 232A* is a *Volkswagen* staff auto. Scale model and photographed by *Günter Sengfelder.*

Loading has begun. The *Volkswagen* staff auto is driving up the ramp into the *Arado Ar 232A's* cargo bay. Scale model and photographed by *Günter Sengfelder.*

Arado Ar 232A* resting on its 11 rows of caterpillar-type fuselage-mounted wheels. Scale model and photographed by *Günter Sengfelder.

A new-looking *Arado Ar 232A* with camouflage. Scale model and photographed by *Günter Sengfelder.*

An *Arado Ar 232A* with its 11 rows of 22 pneumatic tires seen beneath its fuselage. Scale model and photographed by *Günter Sengfelder.*

The *Arado Ar 232A* with its 11 rows of 22 pneumatic tires enabled it to land pretty much anywhere close to the battlefield. Scale model and photographed by *Günter Sengfelder.*

The *Arado Ar 232A* leaving for the battlefield thanks to its caterpillar-type undercarriage. Scale model and photographed by *Günter Sengfelder.*

A nose-on view of an *Arado Ar 232A* seen shortly after takeoff. Scale model and photographed by *Günter Sengfelder.*

A nose-on view of an *Arado Ar 232A* rolling with its full undercarriage on the tarmac. Scale model and photographed by *Günter Sengfelder.*

The *Arado Ar 232A*. Scale model and photographed by *Günter Sengfelder.*

The *Arado Ar 232A's* cargo bay was a rectangular box as seen from this starboard side view. Scale model and photographed by *Günter Sengfelder.*

Operations *Zeppelin* and *Scherhorn*

By July 1944, when *Nazi* Germany's war efforts appeared to be collapsing everywhere, SS *Commander Ernst Kaltenbrunner*, head of the *Third Reich's* Main Security Office, is alleged to have informed *KG 200* commander *Oberst Werner Baumbach* that he needed an *Arado Ar 232B* to fly almost to Moscow. The four motored transport was to land unnoticed, and unload cargo and people. The mission was known as "*Operation Zeppelin*," and its purpose was to assassinate the USSR's dictator, *Josef Stalin*. The assassination was to take place on the 27th anniversary of the October Revolution by a remotely detonated bomb inside a briefcase. It appears that on the night of September 5, 1944, at least two German agents, their baggage, and a motorcycle were loaded aboard *Arado Ar 232B-05* transport with the radio call code *L5+ER*. Its pilot was *Oberfeldwebel* (Sergeant) *Helmut Vierus*. The flying machine came under heavy antiaircraft fire before even reaching their intended landing area. Upon landing the wing of the *Arado Ar 232 B-05* hit a tree and its German crew were captured. The agents, too, were later captured.

Another secret mission involving an *Arado Ar 232B-5* was known as "*Operation Scherhorn*." In the summer of 1944 a German Army group had apparently been caught behind Soviet lines, and their commander, *Oberstleutnant Scherhorn*, was attempting to break through to the West...or so it appeared. According to one story, *Scherhorn* and his men had already been captured by the Soviets and were being forced to broadcast continuous communications requesting that they be rescued. On the other hand, *Oberst Scherhorn* and his 2,000 men may have never existed, but German intelligence accepted the report as true. Initially plans drafted on October 22, 1944, called for six *Arado Ar 232s* from *KG 200* to be put in the air to supply the troops and airlift them out. At least two *Arado Ar 232s* are known to have been sent out, but it all proved to be a waste of time due to fraud and lies.

The *Arado Ar 232A's* cockpit. Scale model and photographed by *Günter Sengfelder.*

The *Arado Ar 232A* in camouflage. Scale model and photographed by *Günter Sengfelder.*

A ground level view of the *Arado Ar 232A* in camouflage. Scale model and photographed by *Günter Sengfelder.*

A typical *Arado Ar 232A,* its port side rear, as seen from above featuring its clean wing surface, cylindrical-shaped tail boom, and dual vertical stabilizers with attached rudders. All the items placed on the tarmac will be accommodated in its cargo bay. Scale model and photographed by *Günter Sengfelder.*

Another view of the same *Arado Ar 232A* seen above. Notice its highly glazed cockpit canopy and the open dorsal hatch aft the *MG 81Z* cannon turret. Scale model and photographed by *Günter Sengfelder.*

Walter Blume's design for a combat zone transporter was achieved in this flying machine. Notice the large wing surface, which could be increased by an additional 25 percent through its "traveling flaps," thus allowing this flying machine to land and takeoff on the shortest and roughest of field locations near the battle zone. Scale model and photographed by *Günter Sengfelder.*

A close up ground level view of the port side of an *Arado Ar 232A*. Notice that its port side main landing gear is without its cover, while the cover rests up against some boxes. Scale model and photographed by *Günter Sengfelder.*

An *Arado Ar 232A*. Notice its port side main landing gear wheel with cover. All 11 rows of its caterpillar-like fuselage mounted wheels are on the ground. Scale model and photographed by *Günter Sengfelder.*

A guided anti-aircraft rocket missile on a wheeled trailer being loaded into the *Arado Ar 232A.* The various types of cargo that could be put into the *Ar 232A's* rectangular box was endless. Scale model and photographed by *Günter Sengfelder.*

The starboard rear side of an *Arado Ar 232A* and featuring its cargo bay loading ramp. Scale model and photographed by *Günter Sengfelder.*

A rear starboard side view of an *Arado Ar 232A* and featuring its wide loading ramp in the full up position. This ramp could be opened in flight, allowing for the offloading of parachutists, as well as pushing out supplies to troops on the ground. The three-wheel dolly belongs to an *Arado Ar 234A* twin turbojet powered reconnaissance aircraft. Scale model and photographed by *Günter Sengfelder.*

The starboard side main wheel of an *Arado Ar 232A* retracted into its wheel well, which had no cover of its own. Scale model and photographed by *Günter Sengfelder.*

The full undercarriage of the *Arado Ar 232A* combat zone transport. Scale model and photographed by *Günter Sengfelder.*

A tail-on view of an *Arado Ar 232A* featuring its dual vertical stabilizers/rudders and shown with its cargo ramp down. Scale model and photographed by *Günter Sengfelder.*

Oberst **(Colonel)** ***Siegfried Knemeyer*. This daring and highly decorated former *Luftwaffe* reconnaissance pilot was pretty much running the *RLM* between mid-1944 and war's end, as *Hermann Göring* slipped more and more into his morphine addiction and fantasy world involving his stolen art collection. *Oberst Knemeyer* was responsible for saving the *Arado Ar 232* from outright cancellation by having it repowered with four *BMW-Bramo 323 R-2* 9-cylinder radial piston engines.**

Plans For A Mixed Wood/Metal *Ar 232B* Transport Designated The *Ar 432*

A follow-on to the all-metal *Arado Ar 232B* transport in early June 1944 was to have been a mixed metal/wooden version known as the *Arado Ar 432. Oberst Siegfried Knemeyer*, chief of new aircraft development at the *RLM*, expressed considerable interest in having *Arado* engineers construct a prototype having wooden wings, control surfaces, and tail section due to *Nazi* Germany's critical shortage of aluminum. All drawings are reported to have been completed for a prototype known as the *Arado Ar 432 A-02*. Pleasing to *Knemeyer* was the fact that *Arado* had taken *Ar 232 B-011* (work number *110 023*) and *Ar 232 B-020* (work number *110032*) to be the first two *Ar 432* prototypes. *Arado* was in the process of replacing *Ar 232 B-011*'s metal wing with a composition wooden wing. In addition, its entire metal tail assembly was being replaced with a composition wooden assembly. It appears that *Knemeyer* issued an order for the series production of the mixed metal/wood *Arado Ar 432* transport on June 10, 1944, with series production to start in October 1945. It is uncertain whether one or both *Ar 432* prototypes were completed by war's end in May 1945, however, subassemblies are known to have been finished for the two prototypes at Eger prior to May 1945.

Further follow-on transports to the mixed wood/aluminum included the *Arado Ar 532, Ar 632,* and *Ar E 441*. Project *Ar E 441* is particularly interesting in that it was proposed to have a wingspan of 197 feet [60 meters], would be powered by six piston engines, and had a multi-landing gear containing as many as 30 wheels.

Arado engineers had suggested a twin-engine amphibian transport known as the *Ar 430* in 1940/1941. Its intended service area was to have been the coastal areas of Africa and the Mediterranean. This amphibian transport was to have been an all metal mid-wing design featuring a crew of two and able to accommodate up to eight passengers. Engineering drawings of the *Ar 430* are reported to have been given to the French aircraft company *Dewoitine* in 1943. They were to have built a prototype and conducted water testing in France. The *Ar 430* project was abandoned in 1944.

No twin engined *Arado Ar 232As* or four engined *Ar 232Bs* are known to have survived more than one or two years post war. It appears that only England was interested in this flying machine, and ferried at least two *Arado Ar 232Bs* to RAF Farnborough for evaluation. Both were later scrapped. All that remains today to provide evidence that *Walter Blume's* combat zone transporter ever existed are a few documents from the former *Arado Flugzeugwerke* and *RLM*, a great three-part article on the *Arado Ar 232* by *Dipl.-Ing. Karl Kössler* published in *Jet & Prop*, *Jörge Armin Kranzhof's* "*Arado*: *History of an Aircraft Company*," a handful of black and white photographs, and now these outstanding color photos of *Günter Sengfelder's* superb and finely detailed *Arado Ar 232A* large scale model featured in this publication.

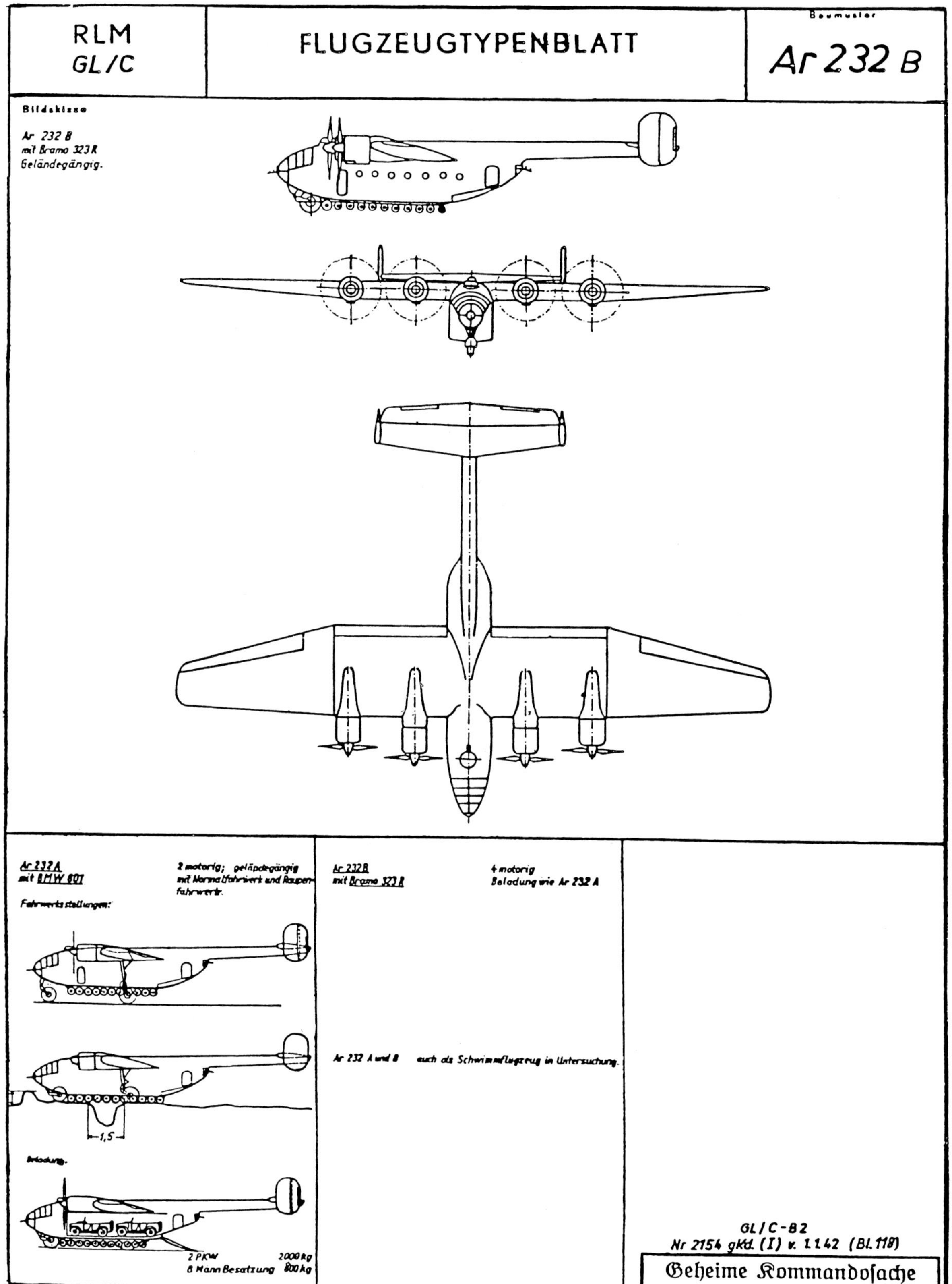

An illustration from *Arado Flugzeugbau* featuring their *Arado Ar 232B*, a four-engined package presented to the *RLM* for construction approval.

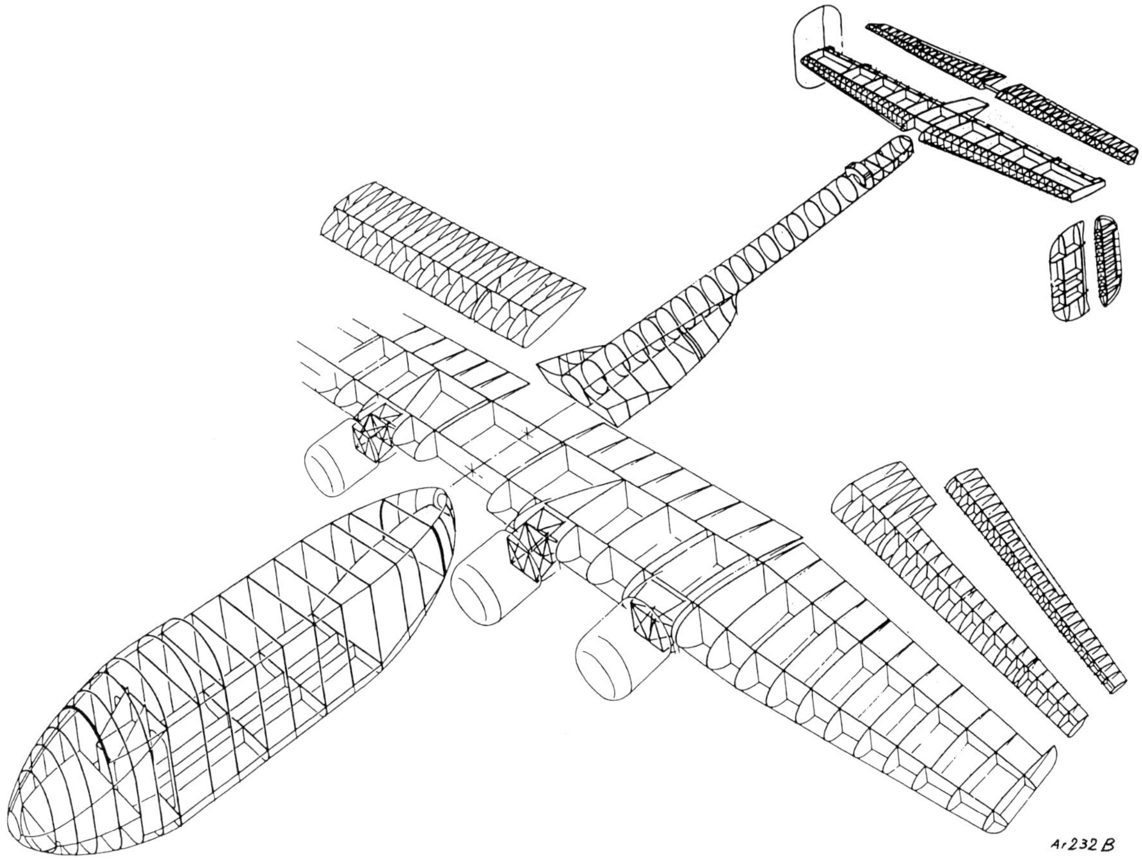

The *Arado Ar 232B.*

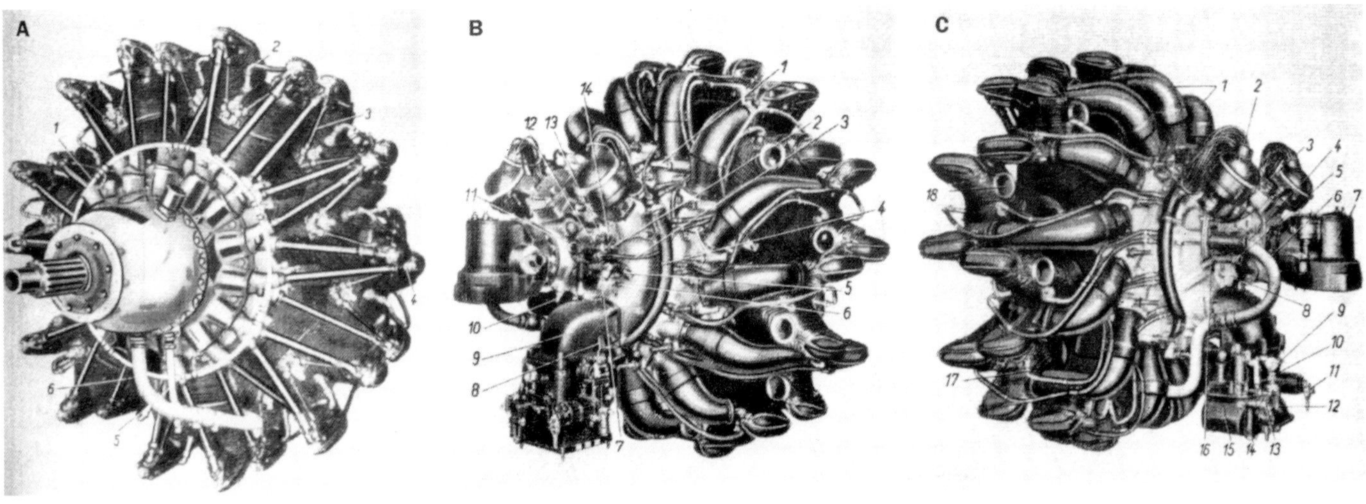

Several views of the *BMW-Bramo 323 R-2* radial piston engine used to power the *Arado Ar 232B.*

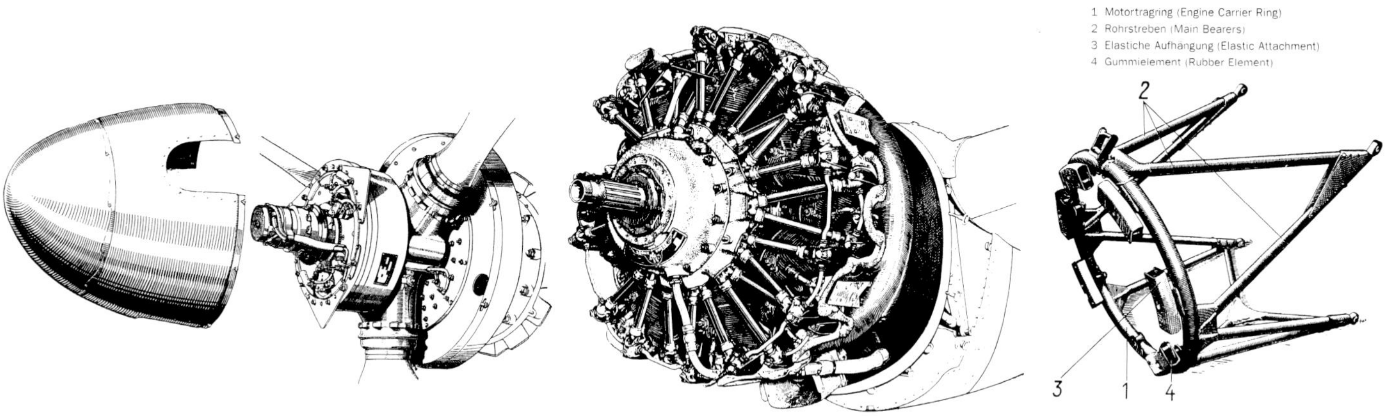

The complete *BMW-Brano 323 R-2* engine assembly as installed in the *Arado Ar 232B*.

The *Arado Ar 232B-01* radio call code *KI+ZT*. It appears that it had suffered a fire in its inner starboard engine.

Bearbeiter: Entwurfsabteilung

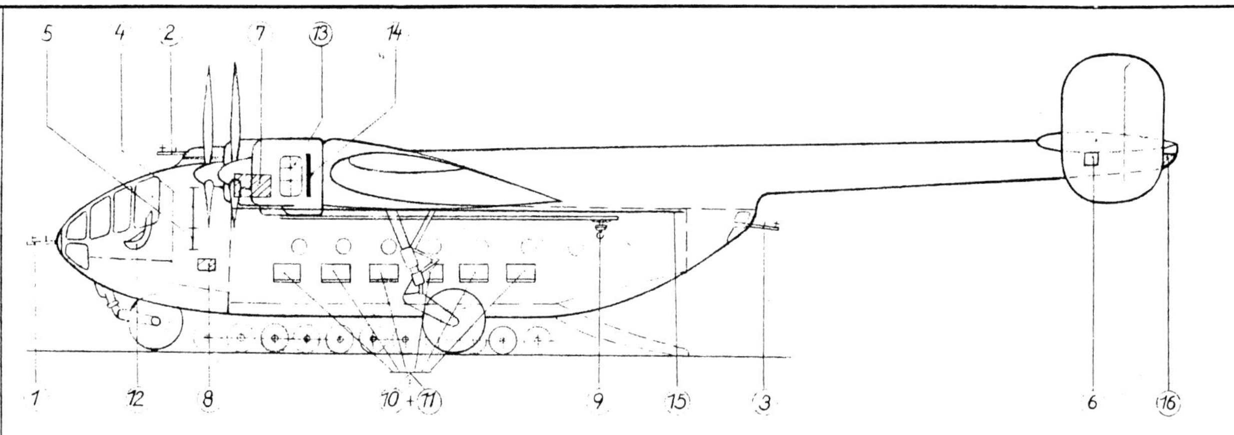

Arado

Transporter

Ar 232 B

Nr.	Rüstsätze	Gewicht kg
1.	A-Stand: 1 MG 81 Z beweglich mit 1000 Schuß	29 28
2.	B-Stand: 1 MG 81 Z beweglich mit 1600 Schuß	78 45
3.	C-Stand: 1 MG 81 Z beweglich mit 2000 Schuß	46 56
4.	Gr. FT-Rahmen (FuG X, Peil G6, FuBl.2)	115
5.	Kl. FT-Rahmen (FuG 16)	30
6.	Kurssteuerung (Rudermaschine i.Heck)	20
7.	Winter- oder Tropen-Ausrüstung	185
8.	Werkzeugtasche, Zurrseile, Boden= anker, Bezüge f. Kabine, Motor usw.	85
9.	Laufschiene und Laufkatze	79
10.	Klappsitze (6 Stück im Laderaum)	30
11.	Ausrüstung für Truppentransport (8 Sitzbänke)	193
12.	Führerpanzersitz (Differenzgew.)	60
13.	Schlauchboot	48
14.	Schlauchbootpanzerung	49
15.	Absprunganlage f. Fallschirmjäger	20
16.	Geschirr für Lastensegler	24

Illustration from *Arado Flugzeugbau* of their four pistoned motored *Arado Ar 232B*.

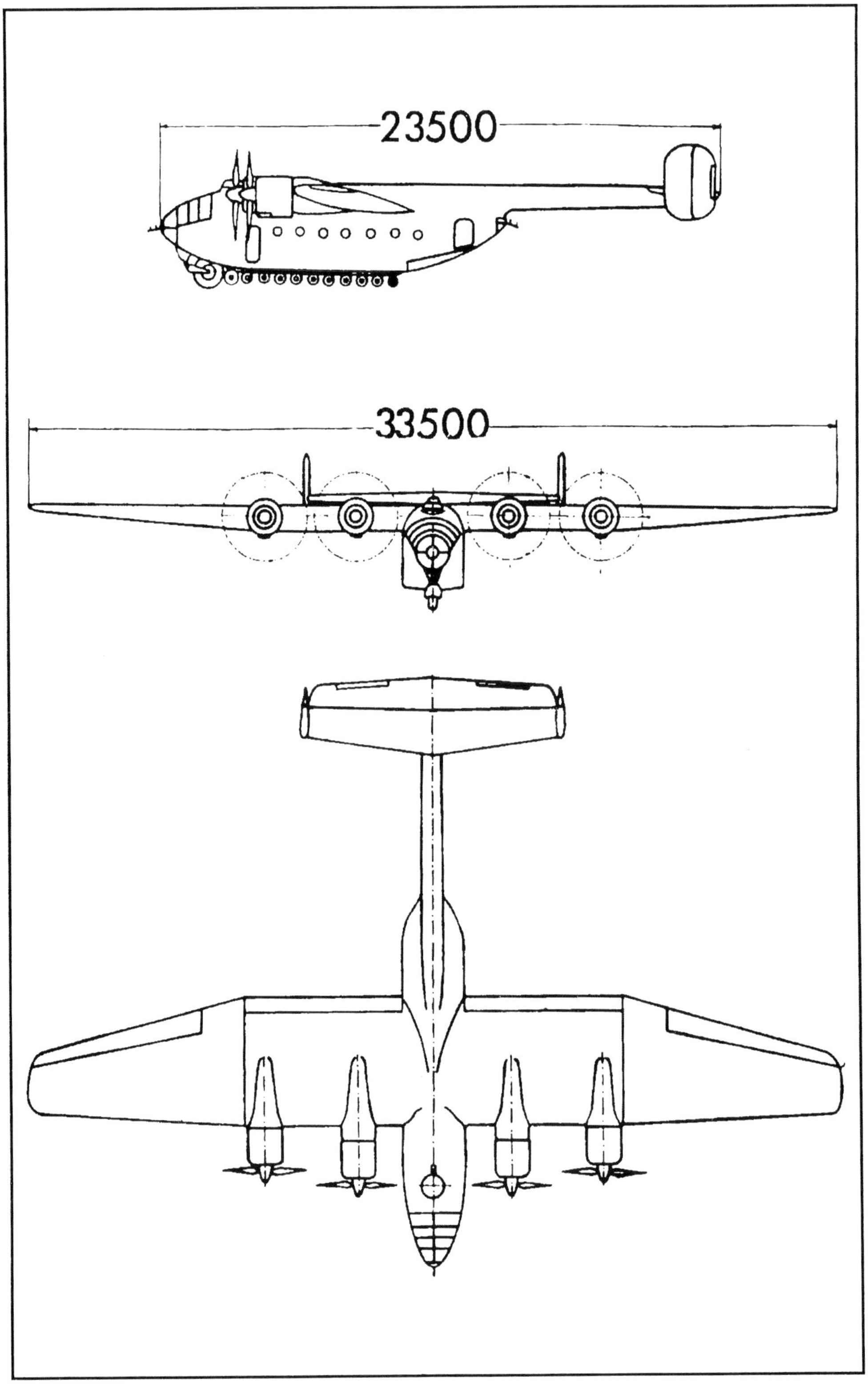

Three view drawing of the *Arado Ar 234B*.

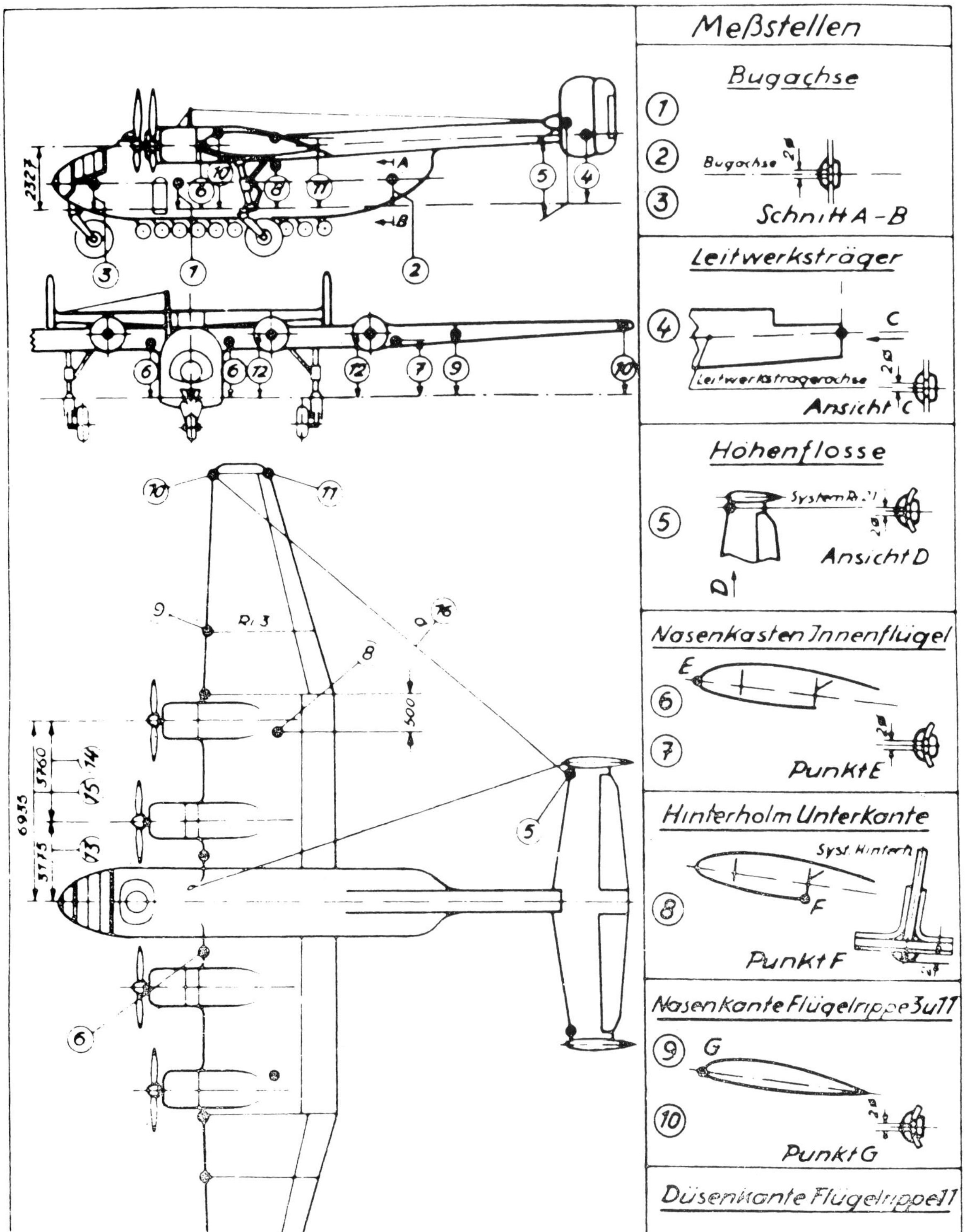

The four motored *Arado Ar 232B*.

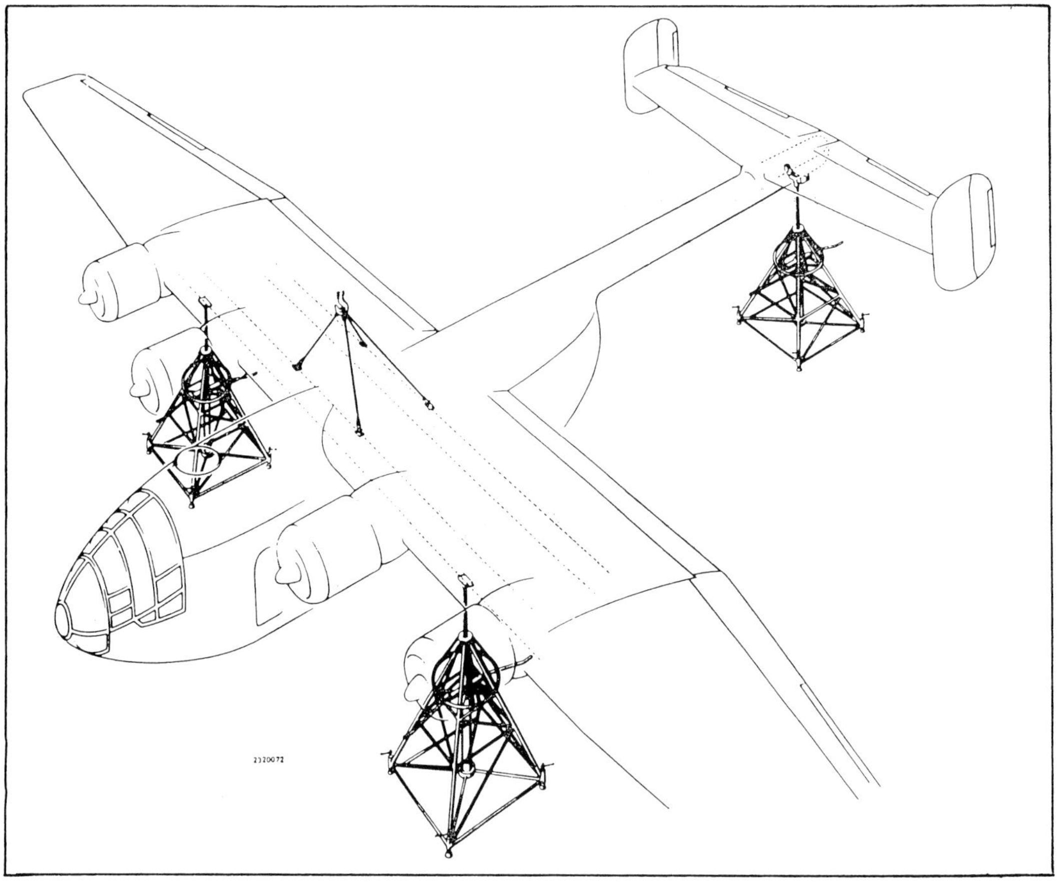

This pen and ink illustration from *Arado Flugzeugbau* illustrates how an *Arado Ar 232B* would be lifted off the hangar floor and then placed on three steel pipe support stands. The *Arado* wing had four lifting eyes positioned just over the fuselage.

***Arado Ar 232B-01*, with its four *BMW-Bramo 323 R-2* 9-cylinder radial piston engines, is seen during final assembly as the first of the "*B*" series. It would later be given radio call code *KI+ZT*.**

The fully assembled and camouflaged (painted) *Arado Ar 232B-01* radio call code *KI+ZT*. This four motored version carried VDM variable-pitch propellers with 11 foot 6 inch [3.5 meter] diameters.

Arado Ar 232B. No radio call code available, although it might be the *Arado Ar 232B-09* with radio call code "*KI+ZT*."

The *Arado Ar 232B-06* radio call code *L5+DR* and belonging to *7/Erg.TG*, from Zilistee. Snow is on the ground, and the transport's engines and cockpit have been covered with tarpaulins. On its forward fuselage is the "*elephant*" motif. To the right of the photo, far in the background is the venerable *Junkers Ju 52/3m* transport.

The "Big Three" shown at their Yalta Conference. Left to right: *Winston Churchill*, *Franklin Roosevelt*, and *Josef Stalin*.

Werner Baumback, commander of the very secretive *KG 200*. Many of its wartime missions remain mysteries.

Oberfeldwebel (Master Sergeant) *Helmut Vienus*, the pilot of the *Arado Ar 232B-05* radio call code *L5+ER* transport participating in *Operation Zeppelin*, which was severely damaged during a crash landing. Courtesy: *Dipl.-Ing. Karl Kössler*, "Schleppversuche mit Lastenseglern," Jet & Prop, 2/96, page 46.

The *Arado Ar 232B-05* radio call code *L5+ER*, which was used in *Operation Zeppelin*, with pilot *Oberfeldwebel* (Master Sergeant) *Helmut Vierus* at the controls when it crash landed at night.

A poor quality photo of the *Arado Ar 232B-01* radio call code *KI+ZT*

***Arado Ar 232B-09* radio call code *J4+UH* belonging to *Trfist 5* and shown here at Keczkemet, Hungary, in May 1944. It is surrounded by members of the Hungarian air force eager to inspect this latest combat zone transporter from *Arado Flugzeugbau*.**

A starboard side nose view of *Arado Ar 232B-09* radio call code *J4+UH*.

A port side view of *Arado Ar 232B-01* radio call code *KI+ZT.* Notice that its large cargo bay landing ramp is down.

The *Arado Ar 232B-09's* radio call code is hard to read, but it appears to still have its factory code of *GD+XP*, which was later changed to *J4+UH*. This combat zone transporter featured twin remote controlled *MG 131* cannons mounted above the cargo bay loading ramp.

An *Arado Ar 232B* painted in a scribble winter pattern camouflage representing some "expressionist" art form. No radio call code available.

What appears to be several wrecked *Arado Ar 232Bs* in a *Luftwaffe* boneyard at Eger. The fuselage in the foreground has a difficult to read radio call code, although *"KI"* is clearly visible, thus making it the *Arado Ar 232B-01* radio call code *KI+ZT*. Notice the four men atop the junked *Ar 232B* in the background, each holding on to a propeller blade.

Near war's end *Oberst Siegfried Knemeyer* was pushing *Arado Flugzeugwerke* to make more of the *Ar 232B's* components out of wood. Although a fully assembled mixed composition *Ar 232B* is not known to have been manufactured, *Knemeyer* was already calling this machine the *Arado Ar 432*. He is shown sitting in the cockpit of one of his favorite flying machines...the *Horten Ho 3d* motor sailplane.

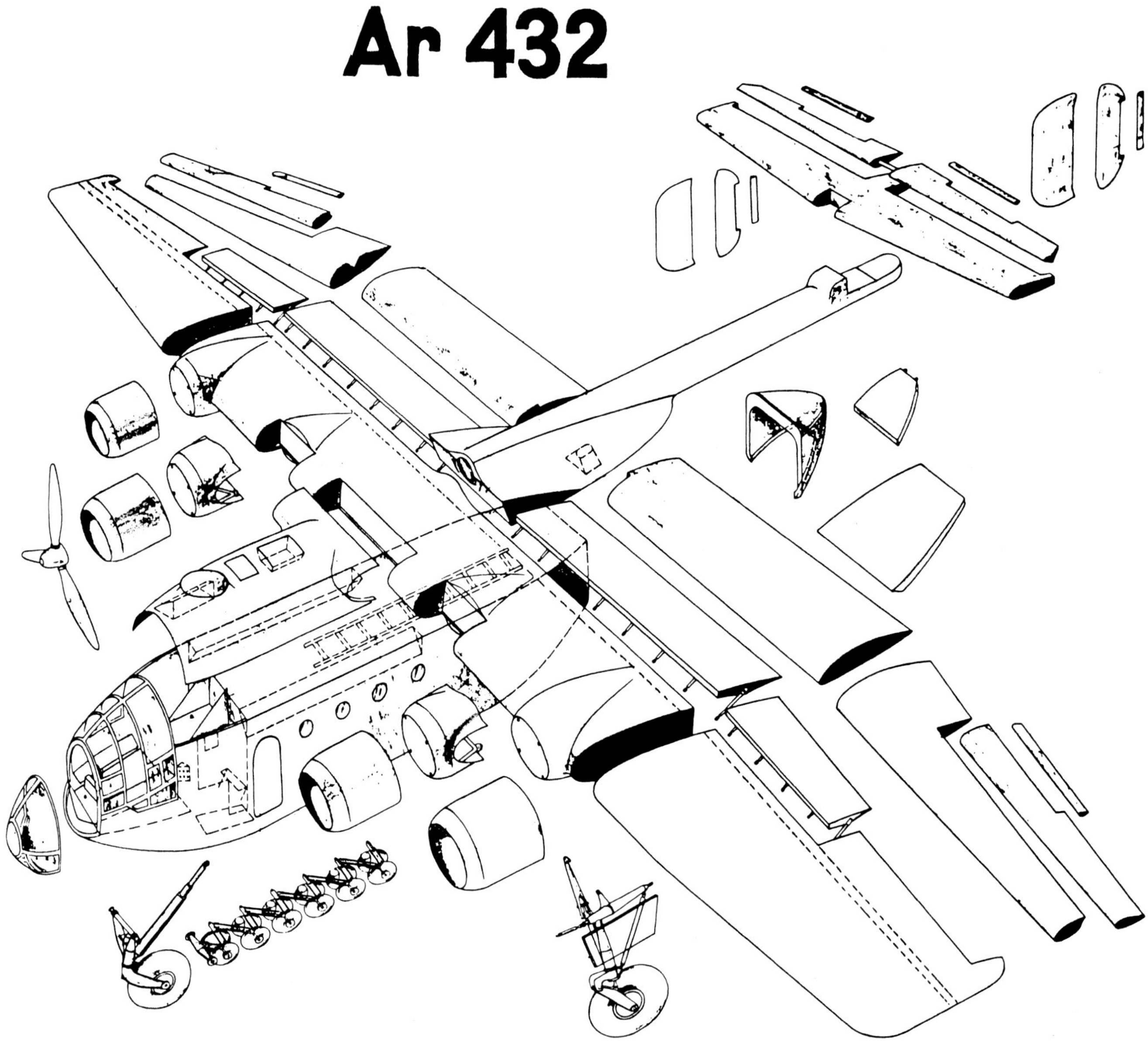

This is the *Arado Ar 432A-O*, the proposed mix composition (metal and wood) version of the *Arado Ar 232B* ordered by *Oberst Siegfried Knemeyer* of the *RLM*. Featured in this illustration are its component parts; some such as the fuselage, which were to be constructed of metal, and others, such as the wing and tail assembly, out of wood. At war's end some of the wooden component pieces had been constructed, but no prototype had been assembled.

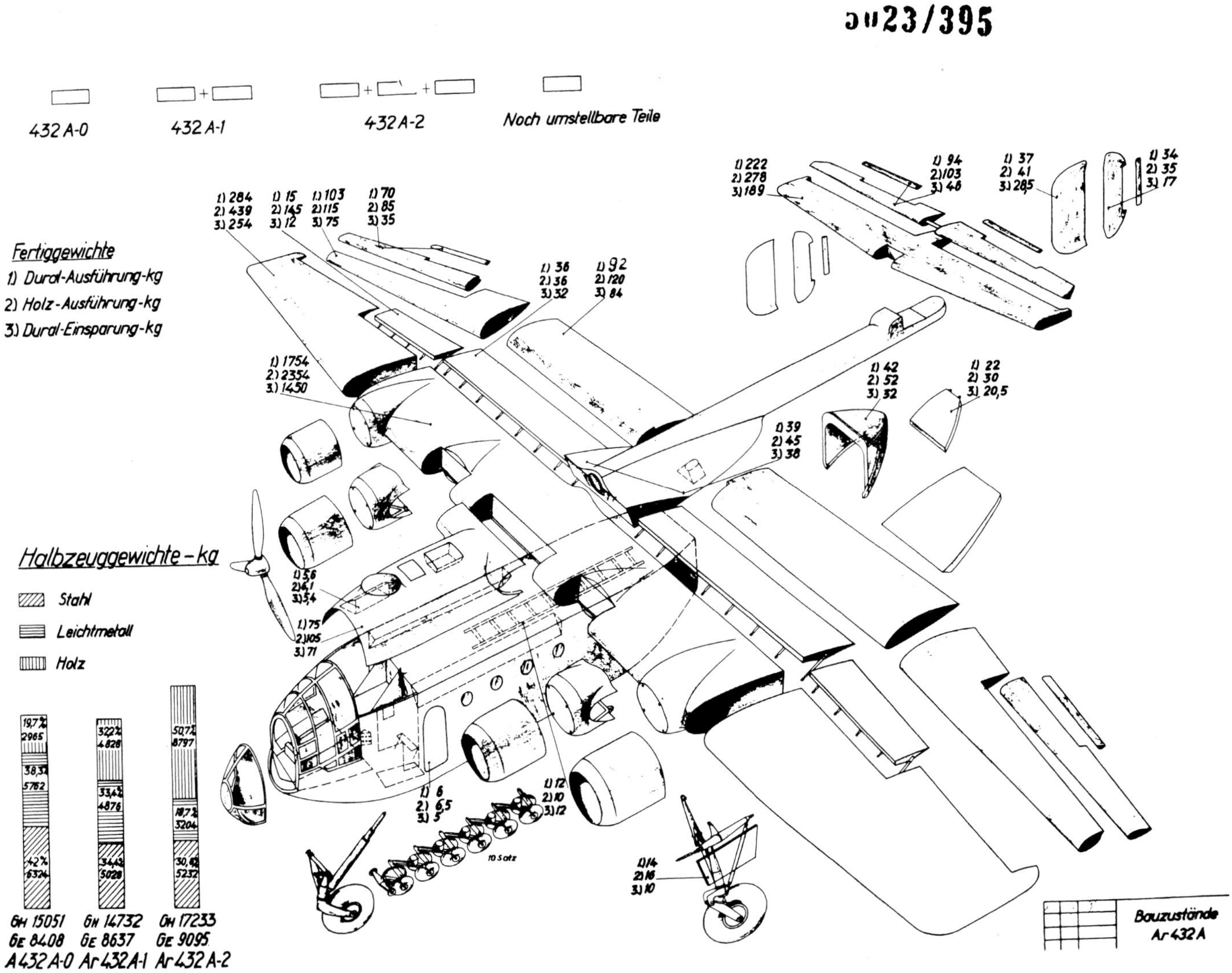

An illustration from *Arado Flugzeugau* of their mixed composition *Arado Ar 432A- O, Ar 432A-1,* and *Ar 432A-2.* This very interesting illustration points out how the mixed composition, including steel, wood, and duraluminum (listed here as light metal) would be used to construct the four motored combat zone transporter.

A starboard side view of *Arado Ar 232B* radio call code *A3+RB* or *G6+YY* post war at RAF Farnborough. An RAF roundel has been painted on its fuselage, however, the *swastika* on its starboard side stabilizer/rudder still remains. The *Arado Ar 232B's* tricycle landing gear oleo struts are in the full down position so that its 11 rows of 22 pneumatic tires are on the ground, too.

***Arado Ar 232B* radio call code *A3+RB* and designated Air Ministry #17 viewed from its port side at RAF Farnborough post war. Notice the "*elephant*" motif remains on the cockpit post war.**

The last known photograph of *Arado Ar 232B* radio call code *G6+YY* as seen in the lower half of the photo. In the foreground to the left is a *Junkers Ju 290.* Immediately out in front is a *Junkers Ju 88*, and there is a *Dornier Do 335* beyond. This photograph was taken at RAF Farnborough prior to being dismantled and boxed up post war. It was never again reassembled, and all containers with their contents were scrapped. *G6+YY*, used in *Operation Scherhorn*, had been captured by the British undamaged at Eggebeck. The last known example of *Walter Blume's Ar 232* series is gone forever.

The proposed *Henschel flugzeug* transporter project. Digital images by Mario Merino.

The proposed *Henschel flugzeug* proposed transport design. Digital image by Mario Merino.

The proposed *Henschel flugzeug* proposed transport design. Digital image by Mario Merino.

Port side view of the proposed *Henschel flugzeug* proposed transport design. Digital image by Mario Merino.

Ground level view of the proposed *Henschel flugzeug* proposed transport design. Digital image by Mario Merino.

Proposed *Henschel flugzeug* transpoer, port rear quarter view. Digital image by Mario Merino.

Ground level fore and aft views of the proposed *Henschel flugzeug* proposed transport design. Digital image by Mario Merino.

TB
EH